Collection Editor: John Denning
Editorial Assistant: Alex Starbuck
Assistant Editor: Cory Levine
Editors, Special Projects: Mark D. Beazley & Jennifer Grünwald
Senior Editor, Special Projects: Jeff Youngquist
Research: Jacob Rougemont
Production: Jerry Kalinowski
Senior Vice President of Sales: David Gabriel

Editor in Chief: Joe Quesada
Publisher: Dan Buckley

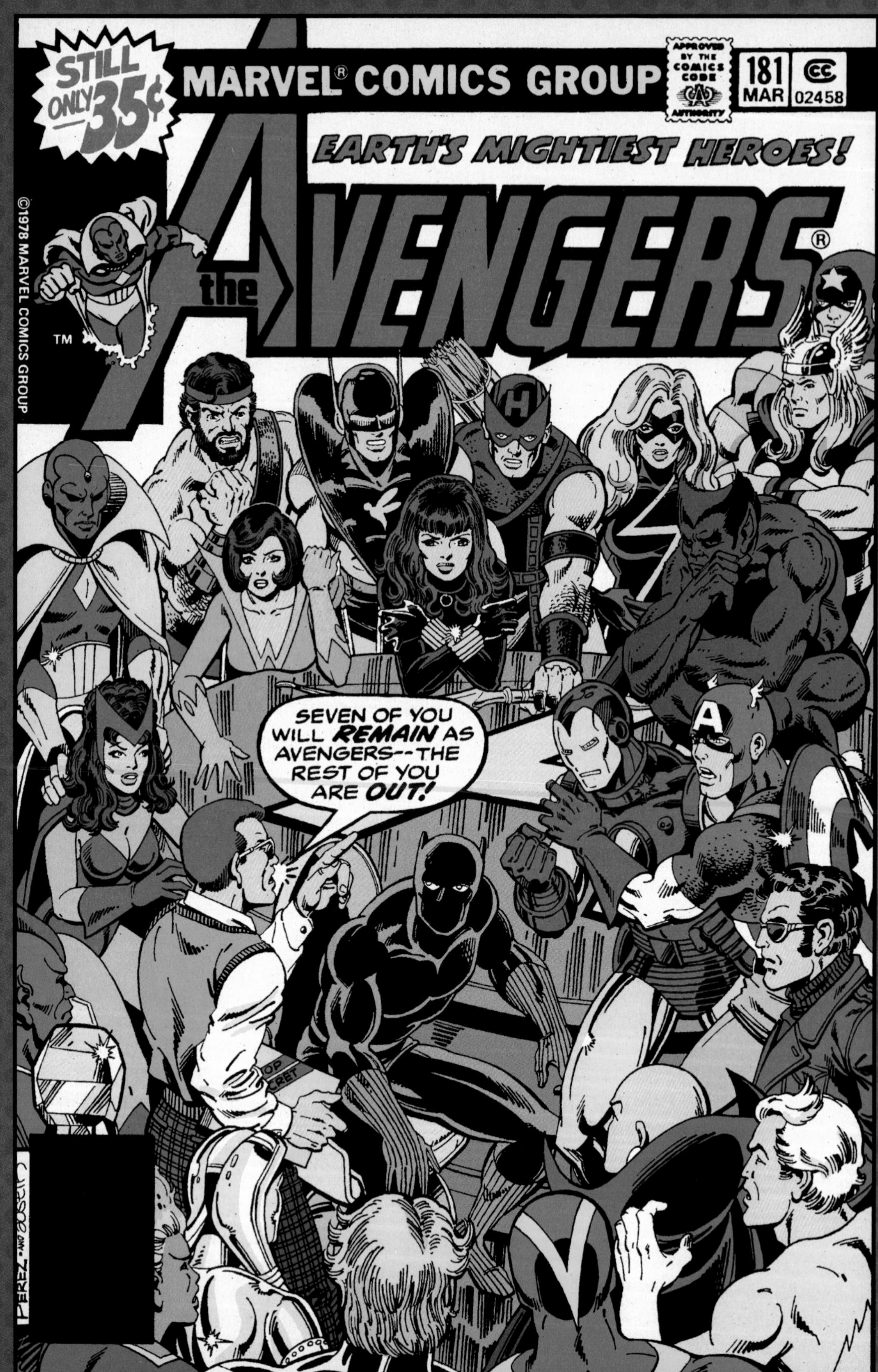
STILL ONLY 35¢
MARVEL® COMICS GROUP
APPROVED BY THE COMICS CODE AUTHORITY
181 MAR
CC 02458
EARTH'S MIGHTIEST HEROES!
the AVENGERS®
©1978 MARVEL COMICS GROUP
TM
SEVEN OF YOU WILL REMAIN AS AVENGERS--THE REST OF YOU ARE OUT!
PEREZ AND JOSEPH

And there came a day when Earth's mightiest heroes found themselves united against a common threat. On that day, the Avengers were born—to fight the foes no single super-hero could withstand!
Stan Lee PRESENTS: THE MIGHTY AVENGERS!
DAVID MICHELINIE WRITER / JOHN BYRNE & GENE DAY ARTISTS / F. MOULY COLORS / ELAINE H. LETTERS / ROGER STERN • EDITOR JIM SHOOTER • EDITOR-IN-CHIEF
ON THE MATTER OF HEROES!
SATURDAY AFTERNOON AT THE REGENCY: WHERE DECADES-OLD EPICS FLICKER TO LIFE, REVIVED... AND REMARKED UPON...
EXIT
EXIT
I DON'T UNDERSTAND, BEAST. PEOPLE FLOCK TO THESE FANTASIES IN DROVES, LIKE THEY'RE HELL-BENT ON ESCAPING FROM THE REAL WORLD. BUT... WHY?
IT'S CALLED "VICARIOUS SELF-ACTUAL-IZATION TRANSFERAL," WONDY. NOW PIPE DOWN AND FINISH YOUR POPCORN!
LG261

BUT AFTER THE CLOSING CREDITS HAVE FADED...
I DON'T BUY IT, BEAST. THERE'S MORE TO AMERICA'S FASCINATION WITH HEROES THAN A BUNCH OF PSYCHO-LOGICAL DEFINITIONS. IT'S ALMOST LIKE --
ERROL FLYNN
KURT WAGNER

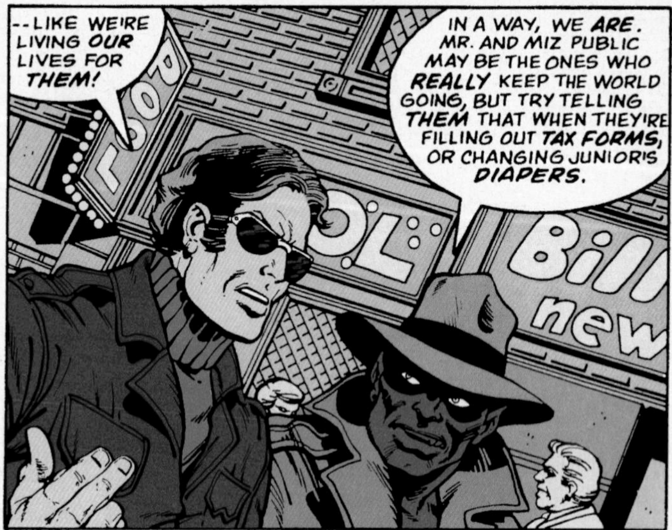
--LIKE WE'RE LIVING OUR LIVES FOR THEM!
IN A WAY, WE ARE. MR. AND MIZ PUBLIC MAY BE THE ONES WHO REALLY KEEP THE WORLD GOING, BUT TRY TELLING THEM THAT WHEN THEY'RE FILLING OUT TAX FORMS, OR CHANGING JUNIOR'S DIAPERS.

FOLKS NEED PEOPLE TO ADD EXCITEMENT TO THEIR LIVES--
--PEOPLE WHO CAN DO THINGS THEY CAN'T--
--THINGS LIKE--
--THIS!
MOMMY, LOOK! A BLUE WOOKIEE!
HEY, GLADYS! IT'S THE BEAST!
OOOH, HE'S CUTE!

SEE?
WELL, SORT OF...
PLAP

...I GUESS IT'S JUST A CASE OF BEING ON THE INSIDE LOOKING OUT. BUT SOMETIMES TAX FORMS AND DIAPERS SOUND MIGHTY GOOD TO ME!

MAYBE I'M JUST NOT CUT OUT TO BE A HERO, ALWAYS ON CALL--

--NEVER KNOWING WHAT'S GOING TO HAPPEN--
INTRUDER ALERT!
BLEET
BLEET
--NEXT...?

DETENTION COILS--HOLD AND SECURE!
HEY! WHAT'S HAPPENED TO AVENGERS' MANSION?!
I DON'T KNOW, BEAST--BUT THESE COILS LOOK LIKE TEMPERED STEEL!

WHICH, SINCE I'M JUST A TAD SHORT OF THOR IN STRENGTH--
SKAK
KRETCH
--DOESN'T MEAN BEANS TO ME!

YEAH, WELL YOU MAY HAVE THE MUSCLES, WONDY--

--BUT THE BUBBLY, BOUNCING BEAST--
POINK
POINK
POINK

--HAS THE STYLE! AND KNOTS TO YOU, DETENTION COILS!
CUT THE CLOWNING, BEAST!

SOMETHING'S VERY WRONG HERE-- AND THAT COULD MEAN THE AVENGERS ARE IN TROUBLE! WE'VE GOT TO GET--

--INSIDE!
KRAKHOOM!

SHEESH! WHEN YOU SUPER-TYPES KNOCK ON A DOOR--
--YOU KNOCK ON A DOOR!

ALL RIGHT, WISE GUY, EITHER YOU TELL US JUST WHAT THE BLAZES IS GOING ON HERE, OR I'LL--

--PUT HIM DOWN, WONDER MAN!
EH? GYRICH! AND MR. STARK?

THIS IS SCOTT LANG, ONE OF MY EMPLOYEES. AND THOSE TENTA-CLES YOU JUST SHREDDED WERE PART OF A NEW SECURITY SYSTEM HE'S INSTALLING--
--A RATHER EXPENSIVE PART, I MIGHT ADD.

NO MATTER, STARK. THEY'LL HOLD UP AGAINST NORMAL INTRUDERS.
NOW, IF YOU'LL HAVE YOUR BODY-GUARD JOIN THE OTHERS IN THE ASSEMBLY ROOM, I THINK IT'S TIME I TOLD YOUR MERRY MEN THE REST OF MY REQUIREMENTS FOR REINSTATING AVENGERS' PRIORITY.
UH, CERTAINLY.

WELL, IT'S ABOUT TIME! WITHOUT THEIR PRIORITY STATUS, THE AVENGERS' EFFECTIVENESS HAS BEEN DANGEROUSLY LIMITED.

I MEAN, SECURITY HAS BEEN A BIT LAX LATELY, BUT THAT MUCH? NO, I THINK IT'S ALL JUST ANOTHER CASE OF BUREAUCRACY AT WORK.

IN FACT, COUPLED WITH THE PROBLEMS I'VE BEEN HAVING WITH SHIELD,* IT'S ALMOST GETTING EASIER TO BREAK THROUGH BRICK WALLS THAN RED TAPE!
*SEE RECENT ISSUES OF IRON MAN -- R.S.

COLD THOUGHTS, MATCHED BY A GENTLE SNOWFALL THAT BEGINS TO LIMN THE ROOFTOPS OUTSIDE, AS...
THAT'S IT, MAC-- AVENGERS' MANSION. THIS CURB OKAY?
DA. THIS WILL BE FINE.

THERE, MY GOOD MAN. YOU MAY KEEP THE CHANGE.
A WHOLE NICKEL? GEE, PAL, THANKS!
TAXI
THE NOTE OF SARCASM IN THE CABBY'S VOICE IS NOT LOST ON THE OLD MAN...

...IT IS, HOWEVER, IGNORED. FOR HE HAS CROSSED AN OCEAN AND A CONTINENT WITH BUT ONE GOAL IN MIND. AND NOW--
--THAT GOAL IS IN SIGHT!

MOMENTS LATER, IN A RATHER CLOSE ASSEMBLY ROOM...
TO BEGIN WITH, I THINK THE MAIN REASON WHY THE AVENGERS HAVE BEEN CONSIDERED A SECURITY RISK SHOULD BE PATENTLY OB-VIOUS--
--THERE ARE JUST TOO BLASTED MANY OF YOU! THE NATIONAL SECURITY COUNCIL CAN'T EVEN KEEP TRACK OF WHO'S COMING AND GOING!

THEREFORE, IN ORDER TO REGAIN YOUR PRIORITY PRIVILEGES, YOU'LL BE REQUIRED TO PARE DOWN YOUR MEMBERSHIP TO A CORE GROUP OF SEVEN.
OTHER OPERATIVES MAY BE CALLED IN DURING EMERGENCIES, BUT WILL HAVE TO UNDERGO SPECIAL SECURITY CLEARANCE AT THOSE TIMES.

I'M THE LEADER OF THIS TEAM --I SHOULD BE THE ONE TO MAKE POLICY. I DON'T LIKE THIS A BIT...!
MAYBE NOT, IRON MAN--

--BUT WOULD YOU LIKE GOING WITHOUT AVENGERS' PRIORITY ANY BETTER?
YOU'VE GOT A POINT, CAP.
NO OBJECTIONS? IN THAT CASE--

--YOUR SEVEN CORE MEMBERS WILL BE--
WHA--?! NOW WAIT JUST A MINUTE, GYRICH! YOU MAY HAVE A LOT OF WEIGHT TO THROW AROUND--
--BUT YOU CAN'T DICTATE OUR MEMBERSHIP TO US! JUST WHO THE HELL DO YOU THINK YOU ARE?

I'M THE GOVERNMENT, MISTER.
ANY MORE QUESTIONS?

GOOD. THIS ROSTER HAS BEEN DRAWN UP BY THE COUNCIL ON THE BASIS OF UNIQUENESS, OF ABILITIES, ESTABLISHED LOYALTIES AND APPLICABLE REGULATIONS.
THE CORE MEMBERS ARE AS FOLLOWS:

"REMAINING AS CHAIRMAN --IRON MAN.

"FOLLOWED BY THE VISION--

"--CAPTAIN AMERICA--

"--THE SCARLET WITCH--

"--THE BEAST--
AWRIIIGHT!

"--THE WASP, AND LASTLY--

"--THE FALCON!"
THE... WHAT?!

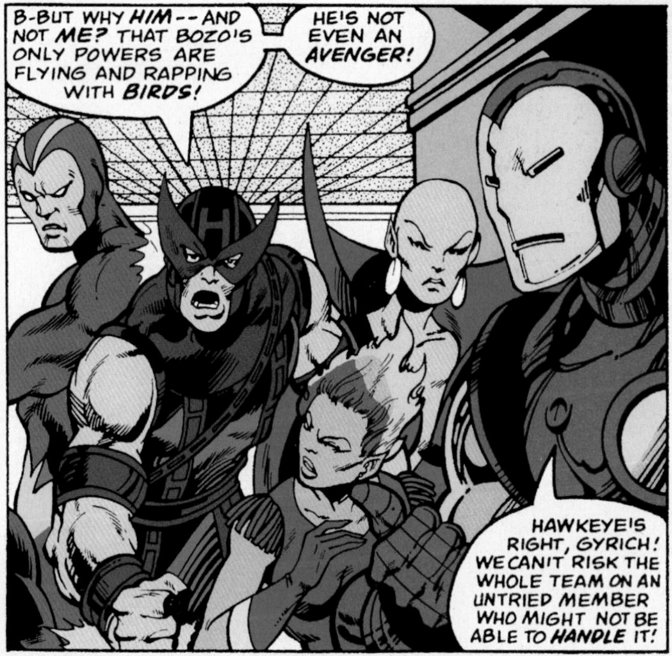
B-BUT WHY HIM--AND NOT ME? THAT BOZO'S ONLY POWERS ARE FLYING AND RAPPING WITH BIRDS!
HE'S NOT EVEN AN AVENGER!
HAWKEYE'S RIGHT, GYRICH! WE CAN'T RISK THE WHOLE TEAM ON AN UNTRIED MEMBER WHO MIGHT NOT BE ABLE TO HANDLE IT!

I'M AFRAID YOU'LL HAVE TO, IRON MAN--SINCE THE BLACK PANTHER ISN'T AVAILABLE. IF THE AVENGERS ARE TO BE SANCTIONED BY THE GOVERNMENT, THEY'LL HAVE TO ADHERE TO GOVERNMENT POLICIES--
--AND THAT INCLUDES EQUAL OPPORTUNITIES FOR MINORITIES!

MINORITIES?! JUST WHAT DO YOU THINK ANDROIDS ARE? AND MUTANTS? AND FOR THAT MATTER--
--SUPER-HEROES?
IRON MAN IS RIGHT! THIS ENTIRE SITUATION IS ABSURD! THE AVENGERS IS AN ELITE GROUP--!

A CRIPPLED ELITE GROUP IF WE DON'T GET THAT PRIORITY BACK, QUICKSILVER! JUST TAKE IT EASY--
--I CAN VOUCH FOR THE FALCON. HE'S A GOOD MAN.

YOU MISS THE POINT, SHIELD-SLINGER! THE AVENGERS SHOULD BE ABOVE THE INTERVENTION OF ANY GOVERN-MENT!
WHY, TO EVEN CONSIDER--

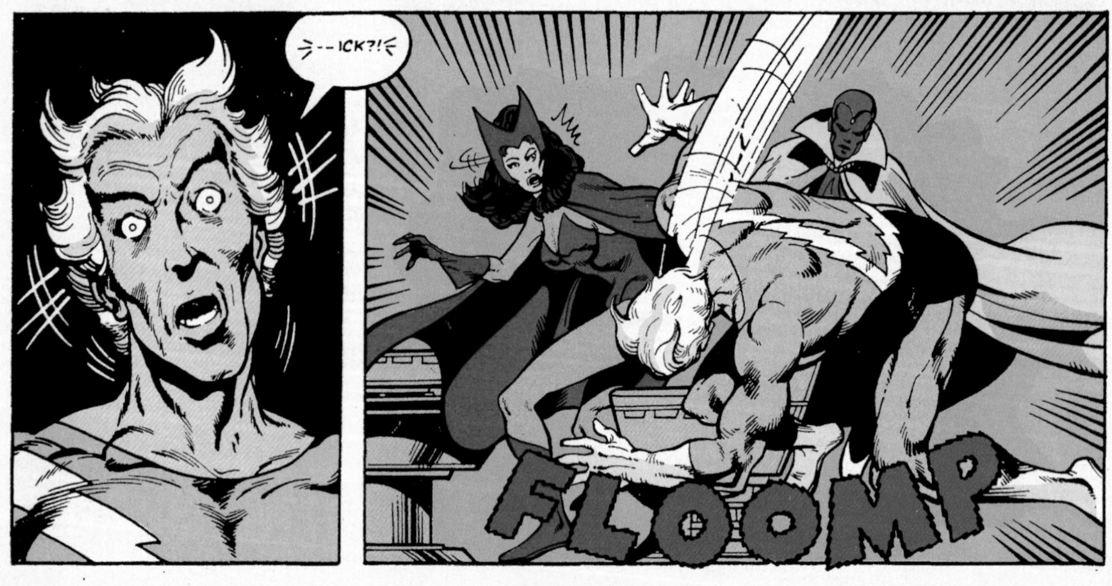
--ICK?!
FLOOMP

HE...HE'S NOT MOVING! HE'S NOT BREATHING!
THOR! GET QUICKSILVER TO THE MEDLAB -- FAST!

I-I'LL CALL A DOCTOR!
NAY, WANDA, I WILL SUMMON A PHYSICIAN! I KNOW WHERE ONE MAY BE GOT WITH GREAT... EXPEDIENCY!

WHAT'S GOING ON?
I'M NOT SURE, GYRICH. BUT QUICKSILVER'S BEEN THROUGH A LOT LATELY-- BEING KID-NAPPED BY THE COLLECTOR, HAVING HIS BRAIN SCRAMBLED BY MOONDRAGON. MAYBE IT WAS JUST TOO MUCH FOR HIM.

OR... MAYBE NOT!

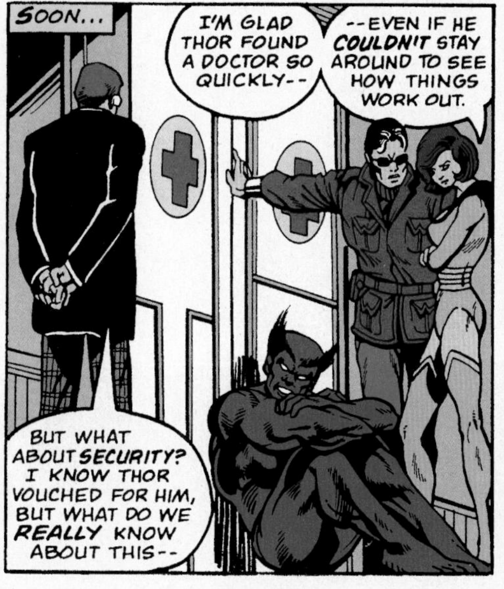
SOON...
I'M GLAD THOR FOUND A DOCTOR SO QUICKLY--
--EVEN IF HE COULDN'T STAY AROUND TO SEE HOW THINGS WORK OUT.
BUT WHAT ABOUT SECURITY? I KNOW THOR VOUCHED FOR HIM, BUT WHAT DO WE REALLY KNOW ABOUT THIS--

--DR. BLAKE?* WHAT'S THE VERDICT?
I DON'T KNOW, IRON MAN. AND I'M AFRAID I WON'T KNOW--
*THOR'S SECRET IDENTITY, RIGHT?--R.

--UNTIL THE RESULTS OF THE **DIAGNOSTIC TESTS** ARE IN.
ALL RIGHT, DOCTOR... I'M SURE YOU KNOW BEST.
THAT I DO. NOW WHY DON'T YOU BOTH TRY TO TAKE YOUR MINDS OFF OF THIS, CONTINUE WITH YOUR DAILY ROUTINE--
--GO SAVE THE WORLD OR SOMETHING. I'LL KEEP YOU INFORMED.

WHILE OUTSIDE, WHERE THE SUN NOW PEEKS THROUGH A GREY COTTON SKY...
MASTER GUARDIANS! I'M SO GLAD YOU'RE STILL HERE!

I'VE PACKED YOU A SMALL **SNACK** FOR THE LONG JOURNEY AHEAD.
THANK YOU, JARVIS. WE ARE MOST **GRATEFUL**.

AND SO ARE THE **AVENGERS**, STARHAWK. WE COULDN'T HAVE DEFEATED THE **ENEMY** WITHOUT YOU.* SURE YOU CAN MAKE IT HOME OKAY?
NO PROBLEM, IRON MAN--SO LONG AS THE **TIME-JUMPER** IN THE COLLECTOR'S ORBITING SHIP ISN'T ON THE BLINK!
*IN AVENGERS #177--R.

WHILE ELSE-WHERE...
RATS! THE OL' DIGS JUST WON'T BE THE SAME WITHOUT YOU, WONDY.
I FEEL STRANGE ABOUT IT, TOO, BEAST.
BUT MAYBE IT'S ALL FOR THE BETTER.

FROM THE TALK WE HAD EARLIER, I'VE DECIDED TO USE MY UNEXPECTED FREE TIME TO TRY MY HAND AT ACTING. IF I CAN GET USED TO PLAYING ROLES ON A STAGE--
--MAYBE I'LL FEEL MORE CONFORTABLE IN MY ROLE AS SUPERHERO!

GOOD LUCK, SIMON WILLIAMS. YOU WILL BE MISSED.

AND ELSE-WHERE...
I DON'T KNOW, JAN. I HAVE BEEN WANTING TO SPEND MORE TIME WITH MY RESEARCH-- BUT THE IDEA OF ONLY ONE OF US BEING AN AVENGER...?
OH, POOH, DARLING. YOU'RE NOT JEALOUS, ARE YOU?

WHY JUST THINK, WHEN I COME HOME AFTER A HARD DAY OF AVENGING, HOW MUCH FUN IT'LL BE--
--GETTING REACQUAINTED?
ANIMAL.

YET AGAIN, ELSEWHERE...
FTHUNG

THOK
THOK
THOK
ONE ARROW, THREE ACES! NOT BAD, CLINT.

AW, I WAS JUST TRYING TO TAKE MY MIND OFF THE FACT THAT I HAVE TO LEAVE--AND AT A TIME WHEN YOU MIGHT NEED ME.

WE'LL ALWAYS NEED YOU, CLINT. AND I'M SURE YOU'LL BE CALLED IN SOON.
BUT TILL THEN... STILL FRIENDS?
"FRIENDS?" HEY, IS A BEAR CATHOLIC?

AND SHORTLY, IN AN ADJOINING COURTYARD...
FAREWELL, AVENGERS. PERHAPS OUR PATHS WILL CROSS AGAIN SOME DAY.
SO LONG, GUYS. GIVE MY REGARDS TO BROADWAY!
HMPH. MOONDRAGON DIDN'T EVEN SAY "GOOD-BYE."

EXCELLENT. YOU'VE KEPT YOUR END OF THE AGREEMENT, AND IN KEEPING WITH MINE--
--I'VE ARRANGED FOR AVENGERS' PRIORITY TO BE REINSTATED IN 24 HOURS.
I ASSUME THE REST OF THE NON-CORE MEMBERS WILL BE GONE BY THEN?

THEY WILL, MR. GYRICH.
NOW IF YOU'LL EXCUSE ME, I HAVE TO CHECK ON PIETR--

--OH.

WANDA! WANDA!

IN MOMENTS...
EASY, VISION. DR. BLAKE'S GOT EVERYTHING UNDER CONTROL.
NO, ACTUALLY, I'M NOT SO SURE THAT I HAVE!

CARE TO ELUCIDATE ON THAT, DOCTOR?
NOT REALLY... BUT I'LL TRY.

IT APPEARS THAT THE SCARLET WITCH'S SYMPTOMS ARE IDENTICAL TO QUICKSILVER'S AND HIS DIAGNOSTIC READOUT HAS JUST COME IN--
--INDICATING THAT QUICKSILVER'S HEART HAS STOPPED BEATING, YET HIS BLOOD RETAINS COLOR AND OXYGEN SATURATION. AND THOUGH HIS METABOLISM HAS CEASED TO FUNCTION, CELLULAR DETERIORATION IS NIL. OR TO SUM UP, WHILE WANDA AND PIETRO FRANK AREN'T REALLY DEAD, GENTLEMEN--
--NEITHER ARE THEY PRECISELY ALIVE!

EPILOGUE: THE LIGHT AFTERNOON SNOW HAS DONE LITTLE TO WASH THE GRIME FROM THE GUTTERS OF THE BOWERY... HAS DONE LITTLE, IN FACT, SAVE TO CREATE SLUSH FOR AN OLD MAN TO STUMBLE THROUGH...
ROOMS
TAXI

...AND TO DRIP ACROSS THE THREADBARE CARPET OF AN ILL-LIT 4TH STREET BOARDING HOUSE...
RING FOR SERVICE
RATES

WE ARE HOME, LITTLE ONES.

DA, I KNOW IT IS A FAR CRY FROM VLADIVOSTOK BUT ANY PLACE IS HOME--
--WHEN WE ARE TOGETHER!

AND THAT IS HOW WE WILL STAY. FOR THOUGH I'VE FORGIVEN YOU FOR RUNNING AWAY FROM ME, NAUGHTY ONES, I CANNOT ALLOW SUCH A THING TO HAPPEN AGAIN.
THAT IS WHY I DO THIS, OUT OF LOVE. I'M SURE YOU UNDERSTAND..

... MY CHILDREN!
NEXT HONOR thy FATHER

35¢
182
APR
02458
MARVEL® COMICS GROUP
APPROVED BY THE COMICS CODE AUTHORITY
©1979 MARVEL COMICS GROUP
EARTH'S MIGHTIEST HEROES!
the AVENGERS®
TM
COSTUMES
THE MANY FACES OF EVIL!

And there came a day when *Earth's mightiest heroes* found themselves *united* against a common threat. On that day, the *Avengers* were born—to fight the foes no *single* super-hero could withstand!

Stan Lee PRESENTS: THE MIGHTY AVENGERS!®

DAVID MICHELINE WRITER / **JOHN BYRNE & K. JANSON** ARTISTS / **D. ALBERS** LETTERS / **BOB SHAREN** COLORS / **ROGER STERN** EDITOR / **JIM SHOOTER** EDITOR-IN-CHIEF

I'M AFRAID THERE'S BEEN NO CHANGE, GENTLEMEN. WANDA AND PIETRO FRANK'S VITAL SIGNS HAVE CEASED-- AND YET THEIR BODIES EXHIBIT NONE OF THE DEGENERATIVE EFFECTS WE NORMALLY ASSOCIATE WITH DEATH!
IT'S ALMOST LIKE--AND I REALIZE THIS ISN'T A TERRIBLY SCIENTIFIC EVALUATION--BUT IT'S ALMOST AS THOUGH...
...SOMEONE HAD STOLEN THEIR SOULS!
HONOR THY father...

I WISH I COULD GIVE YOU SOMETHING MORE POSITIVE, VISION, BUT...
I UNDERSTAND, DR. BLAKE. YOU DO WHAT YOU CAN.

AND IF THERE'S NOTHING MORE THAT I CAN DO, I THINK IT BEST THAT I JOIN THE OTHERS. THE AVENGERS STILL HAVE A JOB TO DO.
GEEZ, WHAT A COLD FISH! HIS WIFE MAY BE DYIN'--AN HE'S WORRIED ABOUT PUNCHIN' A TIME-CLOCK!

WHILE BELOW, IN THE COMPUTER ROOM OF AVENGERS' MANSION...
I'M SORRY I COULDN'T GET ANYTHING FROM MY ANT BUDDIES, IRON MAN.
DON'T APOLOGIZE, YELLOWJACKET. EVEN OUR REINSTALLED DATABANKS HAVEN'T FOUND A CLUE AS TO WHY QUICKSILVER AND THE SCARLET WITCH COLLAPSED ... THIS MORNING.*
*LAST ISSUE--R.

IT'S TOO BAD CAPTAIN MARVEL AND THE REST OF THE COSMIC CLAN HAD TO LEAVE. MAYBE THEY COULD HAVE SENSED SOMETHING.

YEAH, WELL, IF IT WASN'T FOR MR. GOVERNMENT HERE INSISTING THAT WE CUT OUR MEMBERSHIP TO SEVEN BY TOMORROW A.M., THEY'D STILL BE AROUND!
NEED I REMIND YOU, McCOY, THAT ONE OF THE PRIME REQUISITES FOR REINSTATING AVENGERS' PRIORITY IS--
PLEASE!

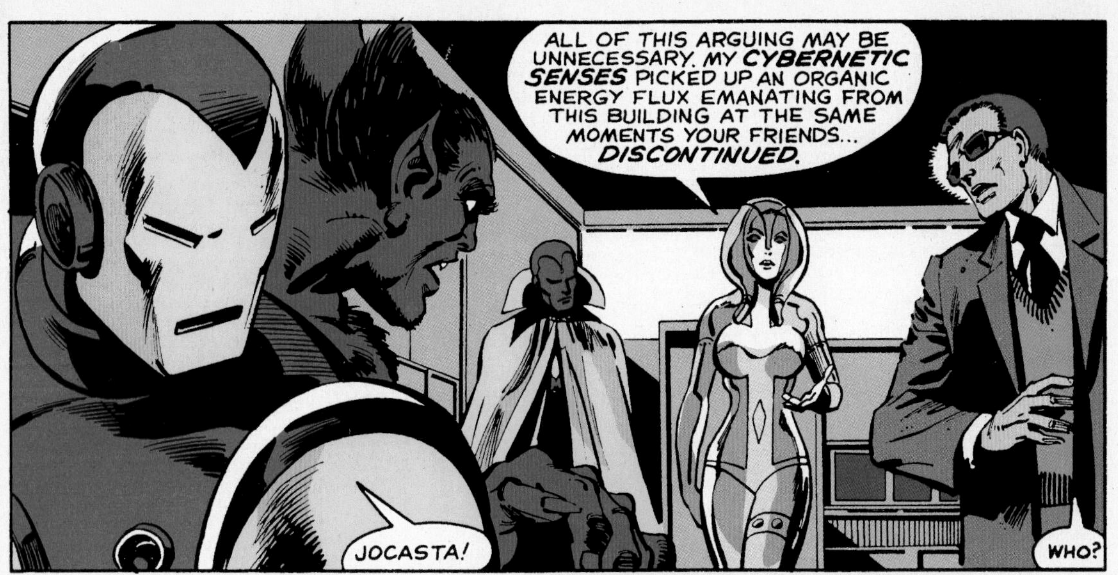
ALL OF THIS ARGUING MAY BE UNNECESSARY. MY CYBERNETIC SENSES PICKED UP AN ORGANIC ENERGY FLUX EMANATING FROM THIS BUILDING AT THE SAME MOMENTS YOUR FRIENDS... DISCONTINUED.
JOCASTA!
WHO?

THE FLUX WAS NOT ELECTRIC IN NATURE, SO YOUR COMPUTERS FAILED TO REGISTER IT.

ROOMS
"BUT WHATEVER THE CAUSE, I'VE TRACED ITS DIMINISHING FLOW SOUTHWARDS, TO THE AREA CALLED THE BOWERY."

HEY! I THOUGHT THIS TIN WOMAN WAS JUST A TROPHY OR SOMETHING!
IF SHE'S INTELLIGENT, SHE HAS TO HAVE SECURITY CLEARANCE!

REALLY, MR. GYRICH, HAS THE GOVERNMENT BECOME SO PARANOID THAT IT REQUIRES SECURITY PASSES FOR MERE MACHINES?
WHY, NO, OF COURSE N... I-I MEAN, THERE ARE EXTENUATING CIRCUM... WELL, THAT IS TO SAY, I--

--I'M NOT QUITE SURE. I'LL HAVE TO CHECK WITH MY SUPERIORS ON THIS.
'BYE!

ALL RIGHT, AT LEAST NOW WE'VE GOT A **TARGET**. BUT SOMEONE HAS TO STAY HERE ON **MONITOR** DUTY IN CASE--
HEY, DON'T LOOK AT **ME**, PAL! COME TOMORROW, I WON'T BE A FULL-TIME **AVENGER** ANY MORE--AN I'M NOT ABOUT TO PASS UP MY LAST CHANCE FOR SOME **ACTION**!

DON'T WORRY, HAWKEYE, I'LL STAY. AFTER ALL--
--IF I'M GOING TO BE A **SUPERSTAR**, I CAN'T TAKE A CHANCE ON HAVING MY GORGEOUS **PROFILE** REARRANGED, NOW CAN I?
YOU GUYS, UH, TAKE CARE, OKAY?
THANKS, WONDER MAN. I GUESS THAT LEAVES NOTHING MORE TO SAY BUT--

--LET'S GO, AVENGERS!

SOUTHWARDS: WHERE A SCRUFFY ROOMING HOUSE IN THE EVEN SCRUFFIER BOWERY PLAYS HOST TO A SCENE BOTH POIGNANT, AND **BIZARRE**...
ROOMS
BUT MY CHILDREN, YOU'LL NEED **STRENGTH** FOR THE LONG JOURNEY HOME!

PLEASE, ANA, JUST ONE MORE BITE? IT'S A GINGER SNAP, YOUR FAVORITE!
ENOUGH OF THIS LUNACY, OLD MAN! I **DEMAND** TO KNOW WHAT YOU'VE DONE TO US!

WE ARE WANDA AND PIETRO FRANK! AND WE ARE NOT YOUR "CHILDREN"!

PIETRO'S RIGHT! OUR PARENTS WERE THE WHIZZER AND MISS AMERICA! WE DON'T EVEN KNOW YOU!
WHY, ANA? I'VE FORGIVEN YOU-- WHY MUST YOU CONTINUE TO TORMENT ME?
THERE USED TO BE SUCH LOVE BETWEEN US! DON'T YOU...

"...REMEMBER? COULD IT HAVE BEEN THAT LONG AGO THAT I, DJANGO MAXIMOFF, WAS SHAMAN TO A TRIBE OF NOMADIC GYPSIES IN CENTRAL EUROPE...?
"AH, YES, LIFE WAS SWEET THEN, AND MY FONDNESS FOR IT WAS EXCEEDED ONLY BY AN UNDYING AFFECTION FOR MY FAMILY--

"--FOR MATÉO OF THE SILVER HAIR, WHOSE SPEED WAS LIKE THAT OF THE CANYON WINDS--

"--AND ANA, WHO COULD WEAVE MAGIC EVEN WITHOUT THE AID OF OUR SACRED TALISMEN, THE NIVASHI STONE.
THANK YOU, ANA. THE NEW WHEEL IS SET!
"OH, DON'T YOU REMEMBER, MY FLOWERS...?

"BUT PERHAPS... PERHAPS IT IS THE BAD TIMES THAT MAKE YOU FORGET, THE TIMES WHEN PREJUDICE AGAINST GYPSIES MADE EMPLOYMENT IMPOSSIBLE--
"--AND I WAS FORCED TO STEAL TO KEEP US FROM STARVATION...

"REGRETTABLY, MY STEALTH WAS LESS THAN PERFECT, AND ANGER FLARED LIKE THE TORCHES OF THE ATTACKING VILLAGERS.

"I COULD DO NOTHING BUT WEEP AS YOUR MOTHER DIED IN FLAMES--
"--OUR SCREAMS MINGLING WITH THE CRACKLE OF BURNING PITCH...

"NOR COULD I BUT WATCH AS YOU BOTH FLED IN PANIC, STUMBLING AND FALLING INTO THE DARK WATERS OF THE MURESUL...

THOD
"IT WAS THE LAST THING I SAW THAT NIGHT...

"OF COURSE, YOU COULDN'T KNOW WHAT HAPPENED AFTERWARDS, HOW I WANDERED FOR YEARS--
"--HOMELESS BUT FOR THE SHELL OF SORROW I CARRIED ABOUT MY SHOULDERS...

"I FINALLY SETTLED IN VLADIVOSTOK, WHERE I CARVED DOLLS AND PUPPETS FOR THE JOY OF...OTHER LITTLE ONES.

"BUT I DIDN'T REALLY CARE ANY MORE. EVEN WHEN I SENSED THAT SOME OF MY CREATIONS WOULD BE USED FOR EVIL,* IT DIDN'T SEEM TO MATTER...
*AS RECOUNTED IN SPIDER-WOMAN #12 --R.

"...UNTIL THE GLORIOUS DAY WHEN TASS RELEASED AN ARTICLE ON THE AMERICAN HERO GROUP, THE AVENGERS--

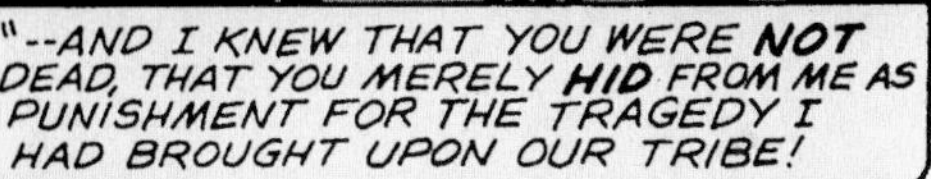
"--AND I KNEW THAT YOU WERE NOT DEAD, THAT YOU MERELY HID FROM ME AS PUNISHMENT FOR THE TRAGEDY I HAD BROUGHT UPON OUR TRIBE!

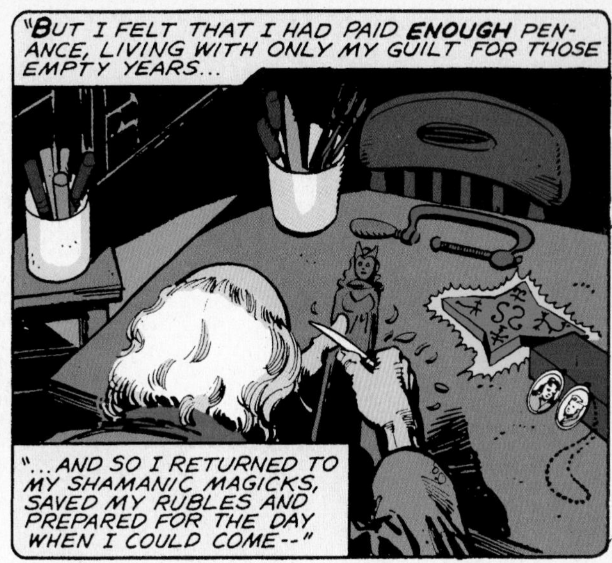
"BUT I FELT THAT I HAD PAID ENOUGH PENANCE, LIVING WITH ONLY MY GUILT FOR THOSE EMPTY YEARS...
"...AND SO I RETURNED TO MY SHAMANIC MAGICKS, SAVED MY RUBLES AND PREPARED FOR THE DAY WHEN I COULD COME--"

--HERE, WHERE I USED THE NIVASHI STONE TO TRAP YOUR ESSENCES IN THESE FORMS. FOR THOUGH I LOVE YOU TO THE DEPTHS OF MY SOUL, MY CHILDREN--I CANNOT ALLOW YOU TO RUN AWAY AGAIN!
BUT WE'VE RUN AWAY FROM NO ONE! IT'S ALL COINCIDENCE, DON'T YOU SEE--?

HUSH, ANA. FINISH YOUR COOKIE. I'VE OTHER THINGS TO ATTEND TO NOW. FOR IT SEEMS THAT--

"--YOUR FRIENDS HAVE COME TO PLAY!"
YOU HANDLE THAT SKY-SCOOTER LIKE YOU'VE BEEN FLYING ONE ALL YOUR LIFE, CAP.
THE CONTROLS AREN'T ALL THAT DIFFERENT FROM A T-16 'COPTER, IRON MAN. I'M JUST GLAD GYRICH GAVE US SPECIAL PERMISSION TO USE IT.

YOU CAN SET US DOWN HERE, CAPTAIN AMERICA.
I SENSE THAT THE ENERGY STREAM EMANATES FROM THAT ROOMING HOUSE.

WHILE ABOVE...
I'M SORRY, YOUNG FRIENDS, BUT ANA AND MATÉO CAN'T COME OUT TODAY. THEY'VE BEEN NAUGHTY.
BUT PERHAPS THE NIVASHI STONE CAN PROVIDE... OTHER PLAYMATES!

CHANTED WORDS, LONG FORGOTTEN BY THOSE WHO CALL THEMSELVES "CIVILIZED", FALL SOFTLY FROM THE OLD MAN'S LIPS... WHILE ACROSS THE STREET, IN A THEATRICAL SUPPLY WAREHOUSE--
COSTUMES

--COLORFULLY ATTIRED PLASTER FIGURES BEGIN TO GLOW, TO PULSE--

--AND TO MOVE!
UH, GUYS...?

SOMEONE WANNA TELL ME I'M NOT SEEIN' WHAT I'M SEEIN'!
PAKRASSH
BUT THAT'S IMPOSSIBLE! THOSE ARE JUST MANNEQUINS!

FWOP
THINK AGAIN, WING-HEAD! FROM THE PUNCH THEY PACK, I'D SAY THEY'RE SOME-THING MORE THAN YOUR EVERYDAY DUMM YOUCH!

THE BEAST IS RIGHT! MY SHIELD JUST LOPPED THAT ONE'S HEAD OFF--BUT IT'S STILL COMING!
SHRATCH

NO PROBLEM, CAP--AT LEAST FOR THE WINSOME WASP!

'CAUSE ALL I HAVE TO DO IS FLY DOWN INTO THE THING'S HOLLOW INTERIOR, THEN INCREASE MY BODY TO ITS NORMAL SIZE AND--

--POWEE!
SKAKLAKT

YEAH, THESE JOKERS AREN'T SO TOUGH! JUST LOOK AT HOW A SIMPLE BOLA ARROW TIES THESE TWO UP FOR THE DURATION!

THAT'S GREAT FOR THOSE, HAWKEYE-- BUT WHAT ABOUT THE SAMURAI THAT'S ABOUT TO CHOP YOUR EGG ROLLS OFF?
WHA--? I-I DIDN'T SEE--!

THAT'S OKAY, BUDDY-- I DID!
AND THEY DON'T CALL THE BEAST A "SWINGER" FOR NOTHIN'!
SWABOTCH

I KNOW I'M SUPPOSED TO BE A SERIOUS, EMOTIONLESS LEADER--
SHRAK
SHRAK
BUT I CAN'T HELP HAVING AN IRRESISTABLE URGE TO SHOUT "DRAW"!

IT APPEARS OUR QUARRY IS AWARE OF OUR PRESENCE. BUT FROM THE EASE WITH WHICH I'M ABLE TO ALTER MY DENSITY AND DISPOSE OF HIS GUARDIANS--

BRAKAKK
--I WOULD SAY HE POSES US LITTLE THREAT!

AFFIRMATIVE, VISION. IF THAT WAS HIS BEST SHOT IT LOOKS LIKE WE'VE GOT IT MADE!
PERHAPS. BUT WE STILL HAVE OUR MAIN OBJECTIVE TO REACH--

--AND THOSE MANNEQUINS' REAL PURPOSE COULD HAVE BEEN TO LULL US INTO OVERCONFI-DENCE.
I SUGGEST WE PROCEED WITH CAUTION.

THERE, IRON MAN! THE ENERGY SOURCE IS ON THE THIRD FLOOR!
UH... UH...
UH...
RATES

WHILE IN A ROOM ON THAT THIRD FLOOR, AN OLD MAN FROWNS-- AND A NEW CHANT BEGINS...

SOON...
THE "RITZ" THIS DE-FINITELY ISN'T!
HMPH! WHAT DO YOU EXPECT FROM SOME TWO-BIT AMATEUR?
I HOPE YOU'RE RIGHT, HAWKEYE.
BUT NEVER-THELESS, WE'D BETTER BE PREPARED FOR THE--

--UNEX-PECTED...?

TSK TSK! YOU YOUNG PEOPLE SHOULD BE ASHAMED OF YOURSELVES! YOU'VE BEEN SUCH A BAD INFLUENCE ON ANA AND MATÉO!

WHY, THEY NEVER WOULD HAVE STAYED AWAY IF IT WASN'T FOR YOU!

AND SINCE IT'S RATHER OBVIOUS THAT YOUR OWN PARENTS HAVE BEEN LAX IN THEIR RESPONSIBILITIES--
--I'M AFRAID THAT I SHALL BE FORCED TO ADMINISTER DISCIPLINE...BY INVOKING THE TRIAD OF GYPSY TOTEMS!
BEHOLD--
ANA? MATEO...?
OH, MY!

"--THE TOAD--
HEY! IT IS THE TOAD!

"--THE SNAKE--
PRINCESS PYTHON!

"--AND THE BIRD!"
HUH? IT'S NIGHTHAWK! B-BUT HE'S ONE OF THE GOOD-GUYS!

DON'T BET ON IT, BEAST! THERE'S SOMETHING VERY STRANGE GOING ON HE--LOOK OUT!
AW, C'MON. SINCE WHEN CAN A HERPETOLOGIST'S NIGHTMARE OUTMANEUVER THE--

--BEAST?!
CROMP

SINCE NOW, YOU BOUNCING BLUE BUFFOON!
CHWUD

CALL OFF YOUR SNAKE, PRINCESS! OR I'LL--
--TURN MY INSIDES TO JELLY? IF I WERE YOU, AVENGER, I'D WORRY ABOUT SOMEONE ELSE'S INSIDES! LIKE--

--MY OWN!

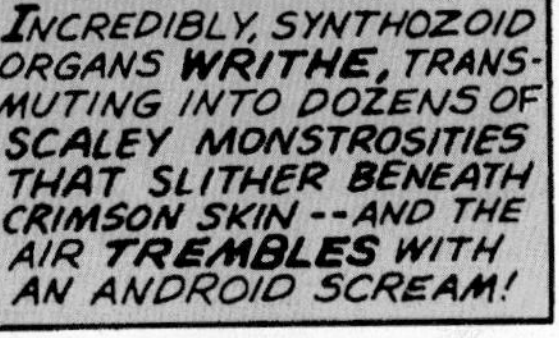
INCREDIBLY, SYNTHOZOID ORGANS WRITHE, TRANSMUTING INTO DOZENS OF SCALEY MONSTROSITIES THAT SLITHER BENEATH CRIMSON SKIN--AND THE AIR TREMBLES WITH AN ANDROID SCREAM!

I DON'T GET IT! PRINCESS PYTHON NEVER HAD SUCH POWERS BEFORE--NOR THE STRENGTH TO STAND UP TO A FULL REPULSOR BLAST!
SHHRAK

WHILE NEARBY...
MISSED, BLAST IT!
KRRITCH
NOT AGH QUITE! WHERE DID NIGHTHAWK GET THOSE TALONS?

HREEEEEE
COVER YOUR EARS, CAP!
THIS SONIC ARROW OUGHT TO PUT A LITTLE SALT ON THAT BIRDIE'S TAIL!

FOOL!
CRACK

SEE HOW MANY ARROWS YOU CAN FIRE WHILE TUMBLING IN A WHIRLWIND!
THAT'S IT, JAN!
FAWOOOSH

HIT HIM WITH YOUR DISRUPTOR BEAMS!
BAH! LITTLE INSECTS ANNOY THE TOAD!
SZZZITT
SZZZITT
SZZZIT
SO THE TOAD WILL DISPOSE OF LITTLE INSECTS--

--AS ONLY THE TOAD CAN!
HUH?!
WHA--?
FWWIP

EEEYUM!
SMEK!

OH, MY GOD! THIS IS INSANE. NONE OF OUR POWERS MEANS BEANS TO THESE CREATURES!
BUT MAYBE SOME UNCONVENTIONAL WEAPONRY WILL--
RRRENCH

--FAIL, TOO! BLAST!
PAKK

LOOK OUT! IT'S A FLYIN'... SINK?!
SKISSSH
HEY, GORDY! P-PASS THE BAG-- QUICK!

WHILE IN A SECOND-FLOOR ROOM...
AW, GEEZ! ≷HIC≶ CAN'T A FELLA GET NO SHLEEP AROUN' HERE?

BONK
BONK
HEY! HAVE A LI'L CONSHIDERATION, WILL YA?
KEEP THE NOISHE DOWN!

HNH? "KEEP THE NOISHE DOWN"? IN LIMBO?
SOMETHING IS VERY UNKOSHER AROUND HERE!
BONK BONK

YOU'RE RIGHT, BEAST! AND I THINK I KNOW WHAT IT IS! THAT GYPSY DAVY CHARACTER MUST BE CAUSING SOME KIND OF ILLUSION--
--HITTING US WITH MOCK MENACES FROM OUR PAST!
CONCENTRATE ON CLEARING YOUR MINDS, AVENGERS!

AND IN SECONDS...
OH, DEAR! OH, DEAR, DEAR!
IT'S WORKING! THE TOTEMS, OUR INJURIES... THEY'RE FADING!
YEAH, AND GEPETTO THERE'S TURNING INTO AN OLD MAN!

NO! I-I WON'T LET YOU TAKE MY BABIES FROM ME! I WON'T!
VISION!
W...WANDA?

MUST GET AWAY! FIND SOME PLACE TO GATHER MY WITS!
C-CAN'T CONCENTRATE ENOUGH TO CAST A SPELL!

PERHAPS IF I LOSE MYSELF IN THIS CROWD, I CAN --
ROOMS

--OH!
WHAT... HAVE... YOU... DONE TO... MY... WIFE?

I... I-I...
NO, VISION! DON'T HURT HIM! HE DOESN'T MEAN ANY HARM!
IT'S THE STONE THAT'S MADE US THIS WAY! PLEASE--!

GRIMLY, A RAGE THAT IS FAR FROM SYNTHETIC WELLS WITHIN THE ANDROID'S EYES, THE SOLAR JEWEL CENTERED IN HIS FOREHEAD BEGINS TO SMOLDER AND...

FWEEEEAK

THANK YOU, DARLING. THANK... YOUUUUUUUU...

THE STREETS ARE STRANGELY SILENT THEN, AS IF SENSING THE LOSS THAT EMPTIES AN OLD MAN'S HEART... A LOSS MADE DOUBLY SHARP BY THE SALTY STING OF MEMORY...
NOT AGAIN. =SNIFF= DEAR GOD... NOT AGAIN.

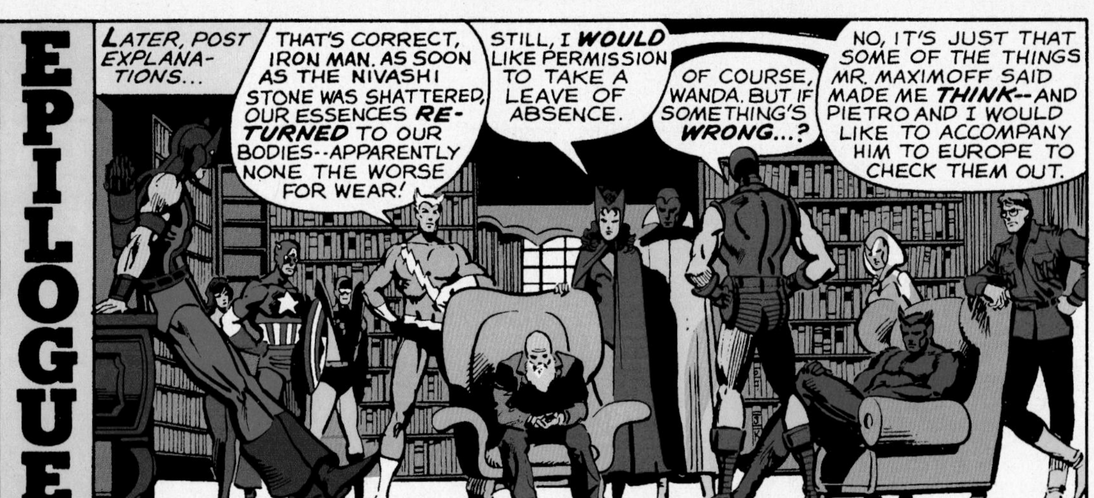
EPILOGUE
LATER, POST EXPLANATIONS...
THAT'S CORRECT, IRON MAN. AS SOON AS THE NIVASHI STONE WAS SHATTERED, OUR ESSENCES RE-TURNED TO OUR BODIES--APPARENTLY NONE THE WORSE FOR WEAR!
STILL, I WOULD LIKE PERMISSION TO TAKE A LEAVE OF ABSENCE.
OF COURSE, WANDA. BUT IF SOMETHING'S WRONG...?
NO, IT'S JUST THAT SOME OF THE THINGS MR. MAXIMOFF SAID MADE ME THINK--AND PIETRO AND I WOULD LIKE TO ACCOMPANY HIM TO EUROPE TO CHECK THEM OUT.

AND ANYWAY, WHAT HARM IS THERE IN GIVING A LONELY OLD MAN A FAMILY... EVEN IF JUST FOR A FEW DAYS?
GOOD LUCK-- TO ALL OF YOU.

WELL, I GUESS THAT'S THAT. EVERYONE'S BACK SAFE AND SOUND AND ALL THE LOOSE ENDS HAVE BEEN NEATLY TIED UP AND GIFT-WRAPPED!
LOOKS LIKE WE CAN ENJOY A LITTLE PEACE, QUIET AND REE-LAK-SA-TION FOR A CHANGE. RIGHT, GANG?

UH...

...NAH, I DON'T BELIEVE IT, EITHER!
≷SIGH≶

NEXT BELIEVE IT OR NOT... THE ABSORBING MAN!

35¢
CC
183
MAY
02458
MARVEL® COMICS GROUP
APPROVED BY THE COMICS CODE CA AUTHORITY
©1979 MARVEL COMICS GROUP
EARTH'S MIGHTIEST HEROES!
the AVENGERS
DORIC
THE ABSORBING MAN LIVES!

And there came a day when *Earth's mightiest heroes* found themselves *united* against a common threat. On that day, the *Avengers* were born—to fight the foes no *single* super-hero could withstand!

Stan Lee PRESENTS: THE MIGHTY AVENGERS!®

DAVID MICHELINIE WRITER / JOHN BYRNE PENCILS / KLAUS JANSON INKER / NOVAK-LETTERS SHAREN-COLORS / ROGER STERN EDITOR / JIM SHOOTER EDITOR-IN-CHIEF

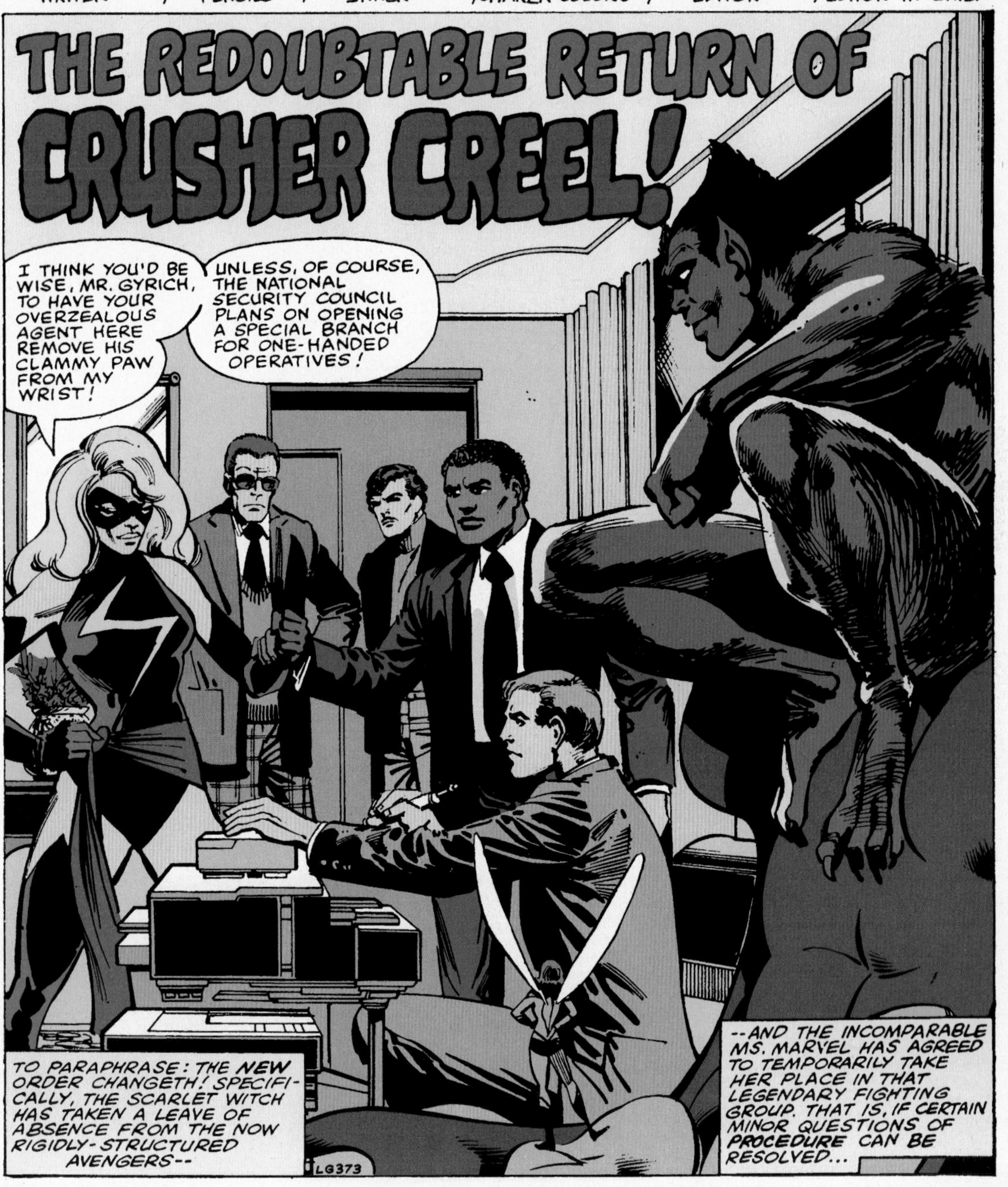

THE REDOUBTABLE RETURN OF CRUSHER CREEL!
I THINK YOU'D BE WISE, MR. GYRICH, TO HAVE YOUR OVERZEALOUS AGENT HERE REMOVE HIS CLAMMY PAW FROM MY WRIST!
UNLESS, OF COURSE, THE NATIONAL SECURITY COUNCIL PLANS ON OPENING A SPECIAL BRANCH FOR ONE-HANDED OPERATIVES!
TO PARAPHRASE: THE NEW ORDER CHANGETH! SPECIFICALLY, THE SCARLET WITCH HAS TAKEN A LEAVE OF ABSENCE FROM THE NOW RIGIDLY-STRUCTURED AVENGERS--
--AND THE INCOMPARABLE MS. MARVEL HAS AGREED TO TEMPORARILY TAKE HER PLACE IN THAT LEGENDARY FIGHTING GROUP. THAT IS, IF CERTAIN MINOR QUESTIONS OF PROCEDURE CAN BE RESOLVED...
LG373

LOOK, LADY, POSITIVE I.D. IS A STANDARD REQUIREMENT FOR JOINING THE AVENGERS THESE DAYS!
OTHERWISE, HOW WOULD WE KNOW IT'S REALLY YOU BEHIND THAT MS. MARVEL MASK?

YOU'D HAVE MY WORD, BUSTER! TAKING FINGER-PRINTS COMPRO-MISES MY SECRET IDENTITY!
ESPECIALLY IF THEY'RE EVER CROSS-REFERENCED WITH MY NASA FILE!
UM, EXCUSE ME?

YES? WHAT IS IT, STARK?
A SOLUTION, I HOPE. HOW ABOUT USING RETINA PRINTS INSTEAD? THEY'RE JUST AS DISTINCTIVE AS FINGERPRINTS--
--BUT LESS LIKELY TO BE RECORDED ELSEWHERE.
HMMM.
WELL...

...I DON'T LIKE IT, BUT OKAY. JENKINS, CARTER:- GO PICK UP THE OPTICAL SCANNER FROM THE OFFICE.
AND BRING BACK THE VOICE PRINT RECORDER WHILE YOU'RE AT IT-- JUST IN CASE!
SHEESH! I'LL BET THAT GUY'S EVEN GOT A TAP ON HIS GRANNY'S HEARING AID!

AND ON THE SUBJECT OF TAPS: IN A NEARBY COMMUNICATIONS ROOM, A SYNTHOZOID HERO HAS TAPPED INTO THE BUILDING'S MAIN TELEPHONE CIRCUIT--
--AND TO A CONVERSATION WHOSE WARMTH BELIES THE STERILITY OF ITS ELECTRONIC TONES...
I KNOW I ASKED THE AVENGERS NOT TO SEE ME OFF, VISION, BUT I COULDN'T LEAVE WITHOUT TELLING YOU GOOD-BYE.
I AM GLAD TO HEAR YOUR VOICE AS WELL, WANDA. DO YOU KNOW HOW... LONG YOU'LL BE GONE?

NOT REALLY. PIETRO AND I HAVE A LOT TO DISCUSS WITH MR. MAXIMOFF.* THAT'S WHY WE'RE TAKING A BOAT INSTEAD OF FLYING.
*SEE AVENGERS #181 & 182 FOR DETAILS.--R.

I UNDERSTAND. AND I HAVE A MESSAGE-- CRYSTAL CALLED FROM THE GREAT REFUGE, ASKING AFTER QUICKSILVER. SHE WAS PLEASED THAT HE'LL BE RETURNING SOON.
SHE MISSES HIM.

I'LL TELL PIETRO. AND BY THE WAY, HE'S NOT THE ONLY ONE WHO'S BEING MISSED... DARLING.

SOMETIME LATER...
WELL, I GUESS I'M A FULL-FLEDGED AVENGER NOW! DOES IT SHOW?
YOU MEAN, ASIDE FROM THAT TELL-TALE GLOW OF PRIDE?
CONGRATULATIONS, MS. M. IT'LL BE A PLEASURE AVENGING WITH YOU!

MOMENTS PASS, SMALL TALK IS MADE, AND THE NEWEST MEMBER OF THE WORLD'S GREATEST SUPERTEAM IS SHOWN TO HER QUARTERS--
--AS THE SPONSOR OF THAT SELFSAME GROUP RETIRES TO HIS...
I HOPE MS. MARVEL WILL BE A VALUABLE ASSET. GOD KNOWS--

--WITH ALL THE RESTRICTIONS THE GOVERNMENT'S HEAPED ON US LATELY, WE CAN USE ALL THE HELP WE CAN GET!
TONY, M'MAN, SOMETIMES I THINK YOU BITE OFF MORE THAN YOU CAN CHEW!

AND SOMETIMES I THINK YOU JUST NEED A GOOD, STIFF MARTINI TO WASH IT DOWN WITH!

BUT THEN...
AW, DAGNAB IT!
WHHRRRRR
EH, LOOKS LIKE I'M NOT THE ONLY ONE WITH PROBLEMS TODAY!

EES NO GOOD, BERNIE. THE HYDRAULIC LIFT, SHE NO WORK NO MORE.
WHRRRRRRRRRR
BLAST! AN' THIS WAS OUR LAST PICK-UP, TOO!

CAN I BE OF HELP, GENTLEMEN?
HUH? WHAZ-ZAT?

I'M AFRAID THIS IS ALL MY FAULT, ANYWAY. I HELPED MR. STARK CLEAN OUT HIS LAB LAST WEEK--
--AND I GUESS YOUR TRUCK JUST WASN'T BUILT TO HANDLE A HALF-TON OF ELECTRONIC SCRAPS!

KRRUNK
FORTUNATELY, THOUGH, MY ARMOR WAS!

THERE. THAT SHOULD DO IT.
SHKRUBALANKKALANG

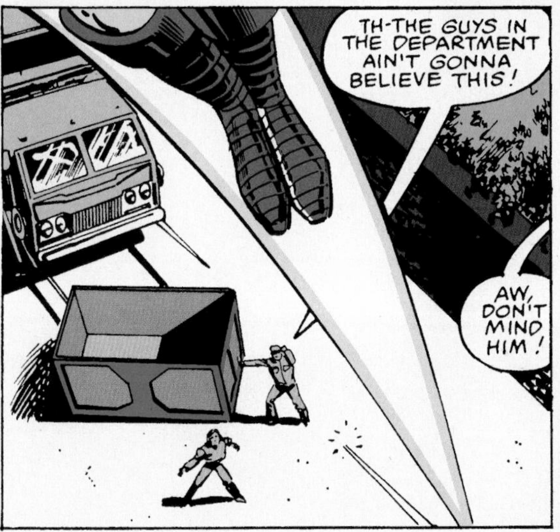
TH-THE GUYS IN THE DEPARTMENT AIN'T GONNA BELIEVE THIS!
AW, DON'T MIND HIM!

THERE ARE A LOT OF WEIRD CHARACTERS HANGING AROUND THIS PLACE!
QUÉ--?

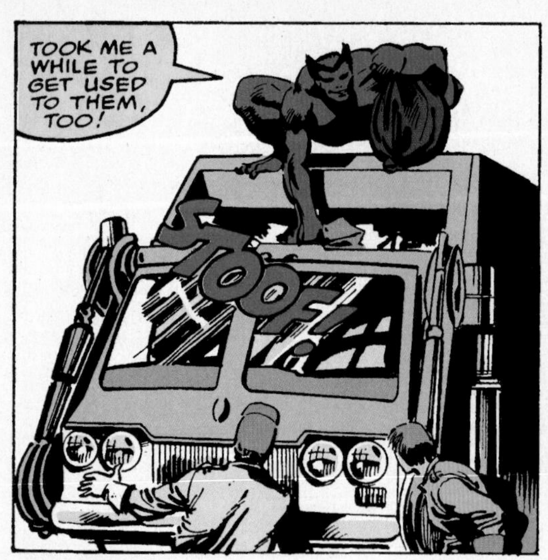
TOOK ME A WHILE TO GET USED TO THEM, TOO!
STOOF!

SEE YOU NEXT TUESDAY, GUYS!
POINK
'BYE!
B-BERNIE--!
DON'T TALK, CARLOS! JUST GET IN THE TRUCK--
--AN' DRIVE!

"AN' DRIVE" THEY DO, AT SPEEDS NOT USUALLY SANCTIONED BY THE DEPARTMENT OF SANITATION...
SANITATION

...UNTIL THE UNCARING TRAFFIC OF THE GEORGE WASHINGTON BRIDGE SLOWS THEM TO A CARBON MONOXIDE CRAWL...

...A PACE THAT LINGERS EVEN TO THE SOLEMN SILENCE AND DECAY OF A NEW JERSEY LAND FILL...
SANITARY LAND FILL SITE

...WHERE...
WELL, WHADYA KNOW? IT'S TOM CHAFFEY, FROM OVER AT AJAX!
HEY, TOM!
WHY, BERNIE TIBBS! YOU OLD REPROBATE!

LOOK, PAL, AFTER WE DUMP THIS LAST LOAD FROM THE NEW FELGERCARB BUILDING, WE'RE THROUGH FOR THE DAY!
WANNA JOIN US FOR A COUPLA BREWS?
SOUNDS GREAT. I COULD USE A LITTLE JOLT!

OH, YEAH? SOMETHIN' WRONG, BERN?
NAW, IT'S JUST THAT THE STRANGEST THING HAPPENED TODAY...
AJAX CONSTRUCTION

BUT HAD THE THIRSTY TRUCKERS TARRIED AT THE DUMP SITE MERE MOMENTS LONGER, THEY WOULD HAVE SEEN SOMETHING EVEN STRANGER OCCUR--

--AS SHARDS OF BRITTLE GLASS SCATTER ACROSS THE PILED-HIGH RUBBLE LIKE SENTIENT THINGS--

--JOINING TO TAKE FORM, TO MOVE...

...TO RISE!
AT LAST! AT LAST!

I'VE WAITED MONTHS FOR ALL MY PARTS TO BE DUMPED INTO ONE PLACE, SO'S I COULD WILL MYSELF BACK TOGETHER!
YEAH, THOSE DO-GOODERS THOUGHT I WAS FINISHED WHEN I TURNED TO GLASS WHILE FALLIN' FROM THAT NEW BUILDIN'-- *
*In HULK #209--Rog.

--BUT THEY WERE WRONG! DEAD WRONG! AN' NOW THAT I'M BACK--
--I GOT ME SOMETHIN' TO DO!

SLOW FOOTSTEPS SHUFFLE THROUGH DEBRIS, AS DARK LAUGHTER FILLS THE FETID AIR. WHILE ACROSS THE EQUALLY FETID HUDSON RIVER...
LOOK, DID ANYONE EVER STOP TO THINK THAT MAYBE I DON'T WANT TO BE AN AVENGER?

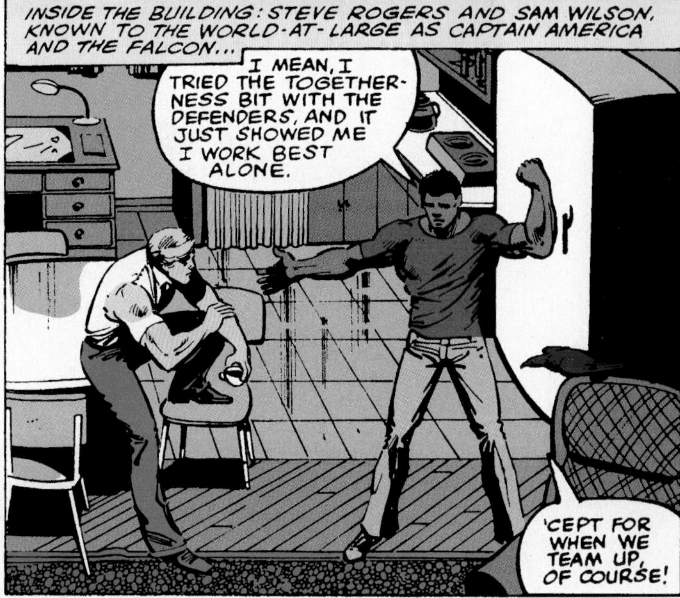
INSIDE THE BUILDING: STEVE ROGERS AND SAM WILSON, KNOWN TO THE WORLD-AT-LARGE AS CAPTAIN AMERICA AND THE FALCON...
I MEAN, I TRIED THE TOGETHERNESS BIT WITH THE DEFENDERS, AND IT JUST SHOWED ME I WORK BEST ALONE.
'CEPT FOR WHEN WE TEAM UP, OF COURSE!

IT'S NOT MY IDEA, SAM. THE GOVERNMENT SAYS WE HAVE TO HAVE MORE MINORITY MEMBERS. AND IF YOU DON'T JOIN--
--THE AVENGERS' PRIORITY PRIVILEGES WILL BE SUSPENDED!

OH, WELL THEN MAYBE I OUGHTA CHANGE MY NAME TO "THE TOKEN", HUH? BLAST IT, STEVE, I'VE PROVEN MYSELF AS A SUPERHERO! AND I DON'T LIKE BEING CHOSEN TO FILL A QUOTA!
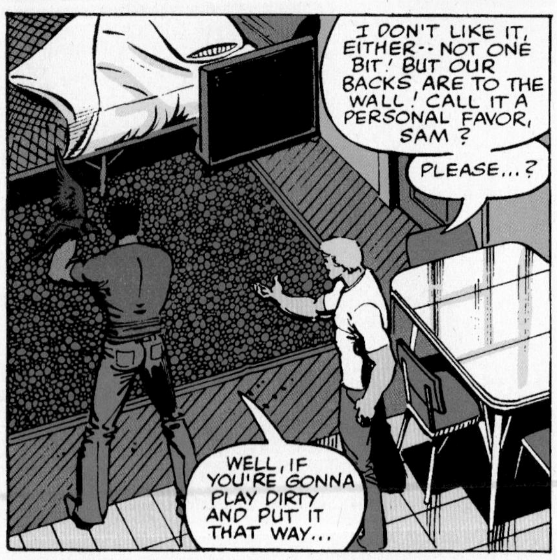
I DON'T LIKE IT, EITHER-- NOT ONE BIT! BUT OUR BACKS ARE TO THE WALL! CALL IT A PERSONAL FAVOR, SAM?
PLEASE...?
WELL, IF YOU'RE GONNA PLAY DIRTY AND PUT IT THAT WAY...

...OKAY. BUT I DON'T DO WINDOWS!
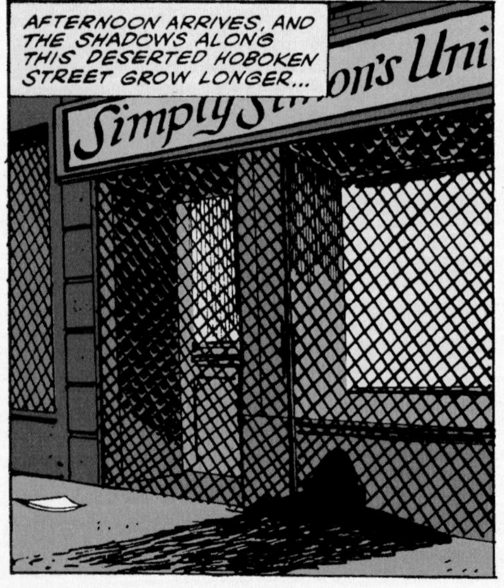
AFTERNOON ARRIVES, AND THE SHADOWS ALONG THIS DESERTED HOBOKEN STREET GROW LONGER...
Simply Simon's Uni

...UNTIL ONE OF THOSE SHADOWS MAKES ITS PRESENCE KNOWN!
NOK
NOK
SANDY
WHATSA MATTER, CAN'TCHA READ? THE SIGN SAYS "CLOSED FER INVENTORY"

"COME BACK T'MORROW."

NO...TODAY!
SKREEKASH

HIYA, CHIPPIE! I'M CRUSHER CREEL! THEY CALL ME THE ABSORBING MAN!
I GUESS YA CAN SEE WHY!

I COME TO "BORROW" SOME CLOTHES!
AN' THESE SLACKS'LL DO FINE-- THEY REMIND ME OF MY OLD PRISON DUDS!
LOOK, FLIPPO, THIS MAY BE HOBOKEN, BUT WE'VE STILL GOT A COUPLE OF HONEST COPS AROUND!
AN' I'M CALLIN' ONE OF 'EM RIGHT NO--

SSSHWAA BRING KRASH

RIGHT NOW, CHIPPIE, I NEED SOME DOUGH!

S-S-SURE! I-IT'S IN THE FLOOR SAFE! RIGHT THERE! I-I'LL GIVE YOU THE COMBINATION--!
DON'T BOTHER...

...LOCKS DON'T MEAN BEANS TO SOMEONE WHO CAN BECOME WHATEVER HE TOUCHES--
--LIKE, F'RINSTANCE, THIS FANCY-SHMANSY STAINLESS STEEL DUMMY O' YOURS!

YEAH, MY POWER AN' THIS CASH'LL BE MY TICKETS OUT!
I MAY STILL HAVE SCORES TO SETTLE, AN' REVENGE'D BE REAL SWEET--

--BUT IT'D PROB'LY BE REAL PAINFUL, TOO!
SKRRRT

HMM, NOT ENOUGH FOR AIR FARE, BUT I SHOULD BE ABLE TO SWING PASSAGE FOR TWO ON A FREIGHTER.
T...TWO?

THAT'S RIGHT. I'M HEADIN' FOR SOUTH AMERICA, WHERE THEY DON'T HAVE NO SUPER-HEROES! THAT WAY I CAN BE THE BIGGEST SONOVAGUN IN THE VALLEY WITHOUT GETTIN' STOMPED ALL THE TIME!
AN' AS FOR TAKIN' YOU ALONG--
--WELL, CHIPPIE, EVEN TOUGH PALOOKAS LIKE ME GET LONESOME ONCE IN A WHILE...
SANDY

THE AFTERNOON AGES SLOWLY, ITS SKY DARKENING WITH A WHISPER OF STORM. WHILE AT A NEW YORK HARBOR...
WANDA!
WHITE STAR LINES

HEY, WANDA!
WHA--CLINT?! BUT I TOLD THE AVENGERS NOT TO SEE ME OFF!

SO WHO'S A FULL-TIME AVENGER? ANYWAY--
--I JUST WANTED TO WISH YOU BON VOYAGE AND BRING YOU THIS YAHTZEE GAME.
IN CASE YOU GET BORED COUNTIN' WHITECAPS!

CLINT BARTON, YOU'RE IMPOSSIBLE!
AND A DOLL, THANKS.

THEN, AS THE GLEAMING OCEAN LINER IS TOWED OUT TO SEA...
THE VISION IS ONE LUCKY MACHINE--
--THAT'S A HECKUVA LADY HE'S GOT THERE!

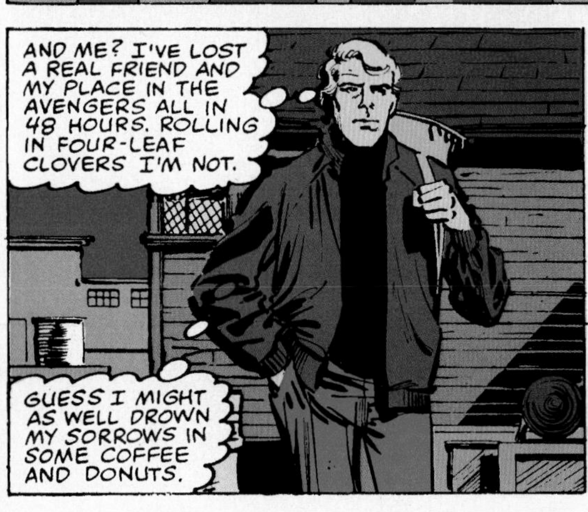
AND ME? I'VE LOST A REAL FRIEND AND MY PLACE IN THE AVENGERS ALL IN 48 HOURS. ROLLING IN FOUR-LEAF CLOVERS I'M NOT.
GUESS I MIGHT AS WELL DROWN MY SORROWS IN SOME COFFEE AND DONUTS.

AH, ON SECOND THOUGHT, UNTIL I FIND GAINFUL EMPLOYMENT, I'D BETTER MAKE THAT JUST COFFEE!

MINUTES LATER, A BLOCK AWAY...
HERE'S A FIVER, BUD. KEEP THE CHANGE.
HUH? BUT THE FARE'S $5.75! WHO DO YOU THINK YOU--

I SAID-- KEEP IT!
WIN
ULP
Y-YES, SIR! TH-THANK YOU, SIR!

WE GOT AN HOUR BEFORE THE SHIP SAILS, AN' I AIN'T EATEN IN WEEKS. WHATSAY WE GRAB A BURGER, CHIPPIE?
THE NAME'S SANDY--
--UH, MR. CREEL.

THIS PLACE IS A REAL SLEAZY DUMP, BUT IT LOOKS CHEAP.
JOBS

C'MON, I'M STARVED!
UHF M-MY COFFEE--! HEY, YOU CLUMSY OAF--

--THAT WAS MY LUNCH YOU JUST SPILLED ALL OVER MY SHIRT! WHAT'RE YOU GONNA DO ABOUT IT?

KWAMM
NOTHIN'.

P-PLEASE, MISTER! DON'T ANTAGONIZE HIM!
ANTAGONIZE HIM?! LOOK, LADY, I MAY TUMBLE LIKE A PUSHOVER--
--BUT I'VE GOT A FEW SURPRISES UP MY SLEEVE!

SO, UNFORTUNATELY, DOES THE "CLUMSY OAF"!

NEXT TIME FELLA, MAYBE YOU'LL THINK TWICE BEFORE --AGH!
H-HE'S TURNED INTO... FORMICA?!
KRAK

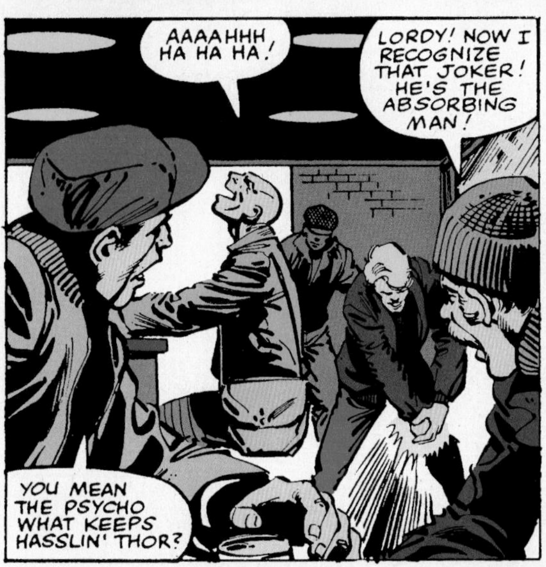
AAAAHHH HA HA HA!
LORDY! NOW I RECOGNIZE THAT JOKER! HE'S THE ABSORBING MAN!
YOU MEAN THE PSYCHO WHAT KEEPS HASSLIN' THOR?

C'MON, GUYS LET'S SAVE THE THUNDER GOD SOME TROUBLE!
W-WAITA-MINIT!
YEAH! THIS JERK'S BIG, BUT HE CAN'T TAKE US ALL ON!

SKRAPASH
HOWEVER, THOUGH THE LONGSHOREMEN'S HEARTS ARE IN THE RIGHT PLACE, THEIR WISDOM--ALONG WITH THEIR ASSAULT--
--IS SOMEWHAT LACKING!

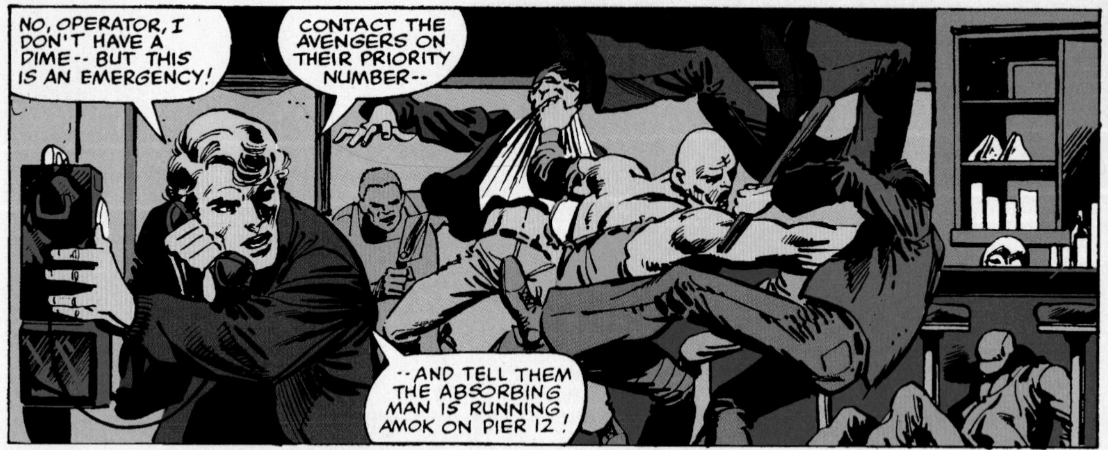
NO, OPERATOR, I DON'T HAVE A DIME-- BUT THIS IS AN EMERGENCY!
CONTACT THE AVENGERS ON THEIR PRIORITY NUMBER--
--AND TELL THEM THE ABSORBING MAN IS RUNNING AMOK ON PIER 12!

MEANWHILE, I'LL SEE WHAT I CAN DO TO KEEP HIM HERE!

THLUBB
BACK OFF, CREEPS! THIS AIN'T NONE O' YOUR AFFAIR!
I GOT 'IM! I GOT 'IM!
YOU KEEP 'IM! YOU KEEP 'IM!

SUDDENLY...
HUH? A NET?!
SHHWIP
SHHWIP

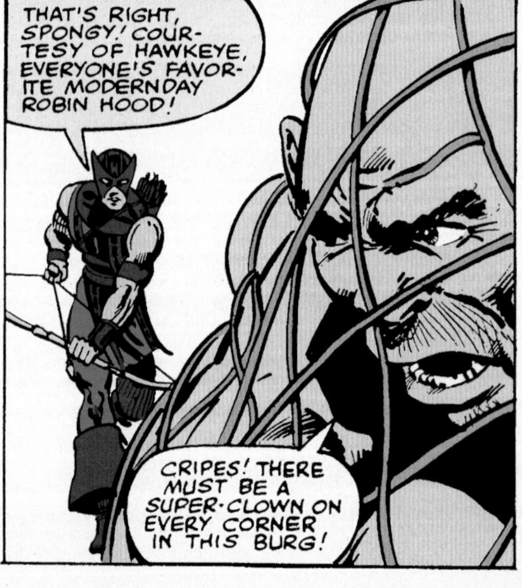
THAT'S RIGHT, SPONGY! COURTESY OF HAWKEYE, EVERYONE'S FAVORITE MODERNDAY ROBIN HOOD!
CRIPES! THERE MUST BE A SUPER-CLOWN ON EVERY CORNER IN THIS BURG!

BUT I AIN'T FALLIN' THIS TIME! SO TURNIN' TO GLASS WON'T HURT ME--

--IT'LL SAVE ME! ALL I GOTTA DO IS FLEX AN' YOUR NET GETS SHREDDED LIKE SPAGHETTI!
MAYBE SO, CREEL--

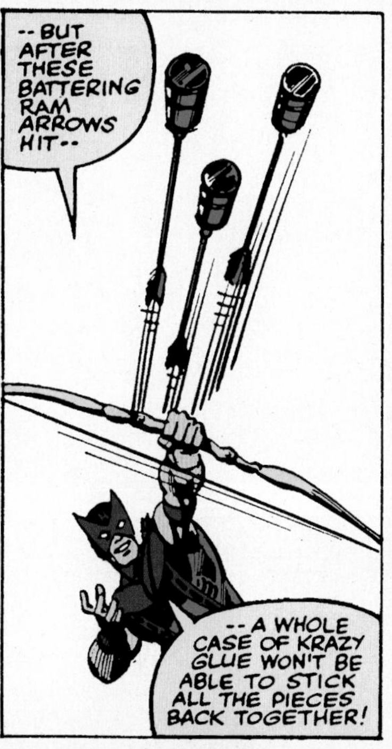
--BUT AFTER THESE BATTERING RAM ARROWS HIT--
--A WHOLE CASE OF KRAZY GLUE WON'T BE ABLE TO STICK ALL THE PIECES BACK TOGETHER!

WRONG, STUPE! ONCE I TOUCH THIS TIRE BUFFER, I'LL ABSORB EVERYTHING I NEED TO--

THAMP
THAMP
--BOUNCE RIGHT BACK! HA HA HA!

BUT THEN...
GIVE IT UP, CREEL! REPULSORS PACK A LOT MORE PUNCH THAN ARROWS--
--AND I HATE THE SMELL OF BURNING RUBBER!
WHO--?!
SSHHRRAK

FOLKS IN THE BIG APPLE CALL US THE AVENGERS, TWO-PLY-- BUT YOU CAN JUST CALL US "FRED AND ETHEL"!
BLAST! CAN'T YOUR KIND EVER LEAVE ME ALONE? EVER?

C'MON, CHIPPIE-- WE'RE SPLITTIN'!

OR SHOULD I SAY... BOUNCIN'!
POMP
HOLEE--!

AFTER HIM, AVENGERS! BUT BE CAREFUL--
--DON'T HARM THE GIRL!

OH, MY! I-I THINK I TOOK TOO MUCH DRAM-AMINE!
SEARCH THE SHIP! EVERY LEVEL! WE'VE GOT TO FIND THE ABSORBING MAN BEFORE--

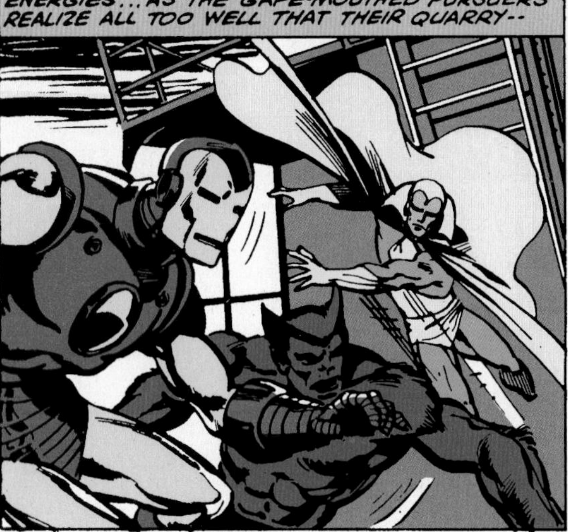
BUT SUDDENLY THE GREAT VESSEL LURCHES, ROCKING WITH THE RELEASE OF UNTHINKABLE ENERGIES... AS THE GAPE-MOUTHED PURSUERS REALIZE ALL TOO WELL THAT THEIR QUARRY--

SHKARRAM

--HAS COME TO THEM!

WHATSA MATTER, HEROES--NEVER SEE A MAN WHO'S ABSORBED THE POWER OF A SHIP'S TURBINES BEFORE? WELL, YER GONNA REMEMBER IT!

'CAUSE I NEVER WANTED THIS--ALL I WANTED WAS TO GO AWAY, BE LEFT ALONE--

--BUT IF YOU WON'T LET GO WITHOUT A FIGHT, THEN I'LL GIVE YOU A FIGHT! AN' IT AIN'T GONNA STOP 'TIL THIS HARBOR RUNS RED--

--WITH AVENGERS' BLOOD!

NEXT ISSUE: DEATH ON THE HUDSON!

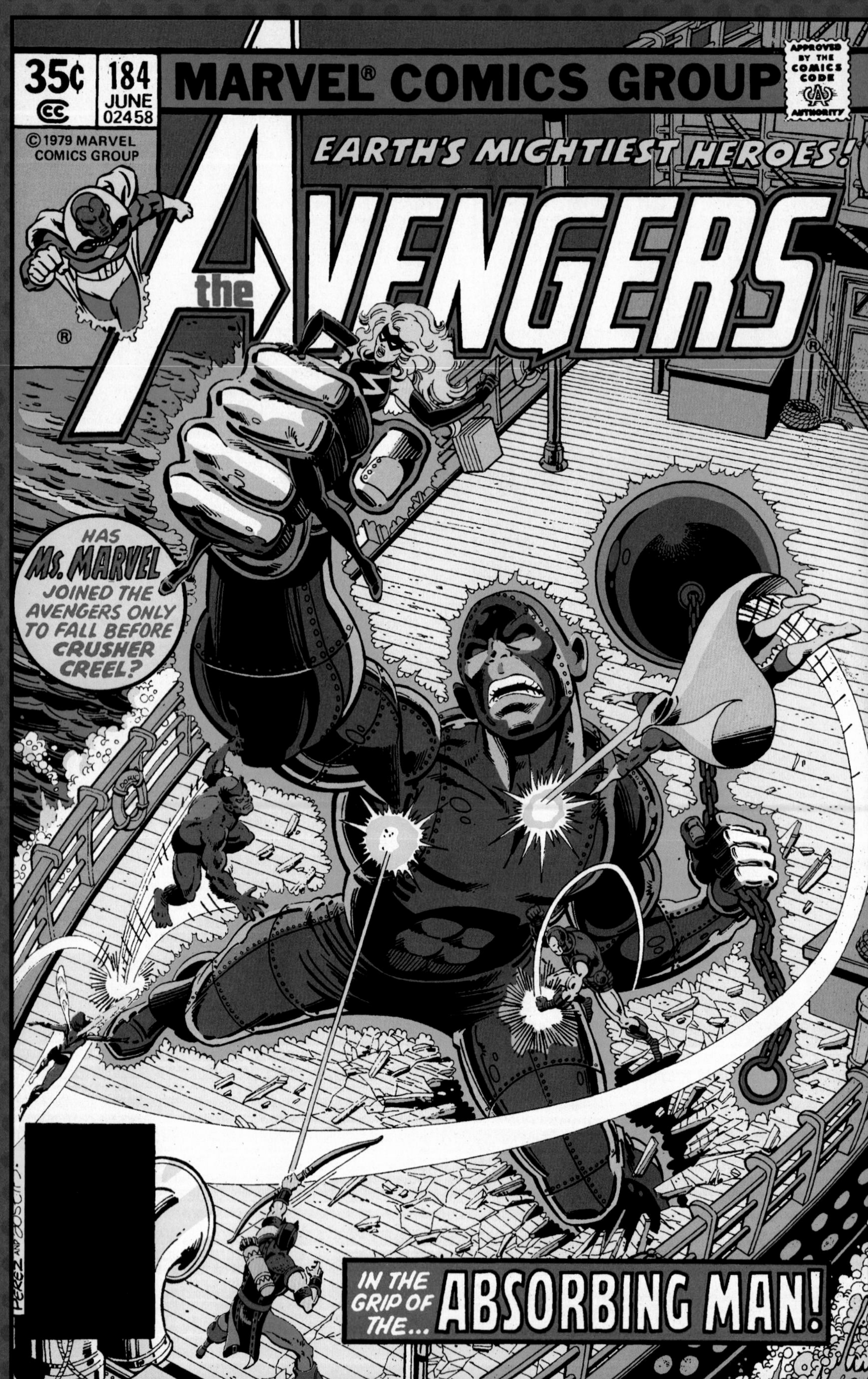

35¢
CC
184
JUNE
02458
MARVEL® COMICS GROUP
APPROVED BY THE COMICS CODE AUTHORITY
© 1979 MARVEL COMICS GROUP
EARTH'S MIGHTIEST HEROES!
the AVENGERS
HAS MS. MARVEL JOINED THE AVENGERS ONLY TO FALL BEFORE CRUSHER CREEL?
IN THE GRIP OF THE... ABSORBING MAN!
PEREZ AND JOSEPH

And there came a day when *Earth's mightiest heroes* found themselves *united* against a common threat. On that day, the *Avengers* were born—to fight the foes no *single* superhero could withstand!

Stan Lee PRESENTS: THE MIGHTY AVENGERS!®

DAVID MICHELINIE WRITER / JOHN BYRNE CHOREOGRAPHY/PENCILS / D. HANDS INKS / B. SHAREN COLORS / D. ALBERS LETTERS / ROGER STERN EDITOR / J. SHOOTER EDITOR in CHIEF

DEATH ON THE HUDSON!

THE GENTLEMAN'S NAME IS CRUSHER CREEL, A.K.A. THE ABSORBING MAN--

--AND HE HAS COME TO NEW YORK HARBOR TO TAKE THIS FREIGHTER TO SOUTH AMERICA, HOPING TO ESCAPE WHAT HE CONSIDERS HIS PERSECUTION BY SUPERHEROES.

HOWEVER, HE HAS BEEN STOPPED IN THAT EFFORT BY THE MIGHTY AVENGERS--

--AND NOW, SEEKING RETRIBUTION, HE HAS ABSORBED THE AWESOME POWER OF AN ENTIRE BATTERY OF ELECTRIC TURBINES!

FOR CRUSHER CREEL CAN ABSORB ANYTHING... EXCEPT DEFEAT!

LG406

LEMME ALONE, WILLYA?
SWA-BASH
WHY SHOULD YOU CARE IF I TAKE OVER SOME PIDDLY-SQUIT BANANA REPUBLIC, ANYWAY?
JUST GO AWAY!

THAT'S EASY, BUNKY.
CAN YOU IMAGINE WHAT WOULD HAPPEN TO THE PRICE OF BANANAS IF YOU DID?
THWAK
LITTLE WITCH!

WHOONF!
I DON'T EVEN NEED MY BALL AN' CHAIN TO TAKE CARE O' YOU!
I'LL JUST SHOW YA WHY THEY CALL ME CRUSHER CREEL!

NOW, BEAT IT!

OH, NO! MS. MARVEL'S STUNNED! BUT I CAN'T LET HER DROWN ON HER FIRST MISSION AS AN OFFICIAL AVENGER! SOOO...

GEE-
RON-
EE-
MO!

HOWEVER, WHILE THE BEAST'S COURAGE AND INTENTIONS ARE OF THE HIGHEST ORDER--
PLUPSH
--HIS SWIMMING SKILLS ARE NOT!

THOUGH HE SINKS REAL WELL...!

BLAST YOU, CREEL!
WHICH IS JUST WHAT I'D LIKE TO DO--EXCEPT THAT MY STINGS ARE USELESS AGAINST HIS ARMORED HIDE!

JUST WAIT'LL I GET MY BALL AN' CHAIN, INSECT! I'LL SWAT YA FASTER THAN--EH?
IS THIS WHAT YOU'RE LOOKING FOR, VILLAIN? VERY WELL, THEN--

--YOU MAY HAVE IT BACK!
FWOMB

JUST KEEP IT UP, REDSKIN! YA CAN'T HOLD ME OFF FOREVER!
WHUMB
HE'S NOT SHOOTING FOR "FOREVER", PAL--JUST "LONG ENOUGH"!

VISION WAS PROVIDING A DIVERSION FOR ME TO GET BEHIND YOU! BECAUSE WHILE I DON'T HAVE YOUR NATURAL ABSORBING ABILITIES--
--I DO HAVE RECHARGING CIRCUITS THAT ALLOW ME TO SIPHON OFF YOUR ELECTRICAL POWER!

AND THIS IRON MAN DOES, DRAWING MEGA-ERG AFTER MEGA-ERG OF INCREDIBLE TURBINE ENERGY INTO THE TRANSISTORIZED SKIN OF HIS ARMOR--
S... STOP IT...!

--UNTIL THE ABSORBING MAN BEGINS TO FALTER, TO SHRINK... AND TO STRUGGLE DESPERATELY!
GET OFF--!

WHILE NEARBY...
THANKS, ANYWAY, BEAST--BUT THAT DIP IN THE WATER WAS ALL I NEEDED TO REVIVE ME! YOU OKAY?
JUST KOF EXCEPTIONALLY EMBARRASSED! I--

--UH-OH! LOOKS LIKE THINGS HAVE GOTTEN PRETTY HAIRY WHILE WE WERE TRYING TO DRINK THE RIVER!

THAT THEY HAVE! FOR IN HIS STRUGGLES, THE NEARLY NORMAL-SIZED ABSORBING MAN HAS GAINED A POSITION OF LEVERAGE. AND NOW...
THERE!

NICE TRY, TIN-HEAD! BUT IT LOOKS LIKE I'VE GOT THE ADVANTAGE NOW, HUH.

HUH?!
ADVANTAGE IS ONE THING, CREEL--

KRUNCHASH
"--BUT SKILL IS QUITE ANOTHER!"

THERE HE IS, MS. M! DROP ME!
UH, ARE YOU SURE THIS IS GOING TO WORK, BEAST?

AM I SURE? HEY, IS GEORGIE JESSEL JEWISH?

IRON MAN! WHAT--?
STAY BACK! MY STORAGE COM-PONENTS HAVE NEVER HAD TO COPE WITH THIS MUCH POWER BEFORE!
I'VE GOT TO GET OUT OF THE AT-MOSPHERE, DISCHARGE THE EXCESS!

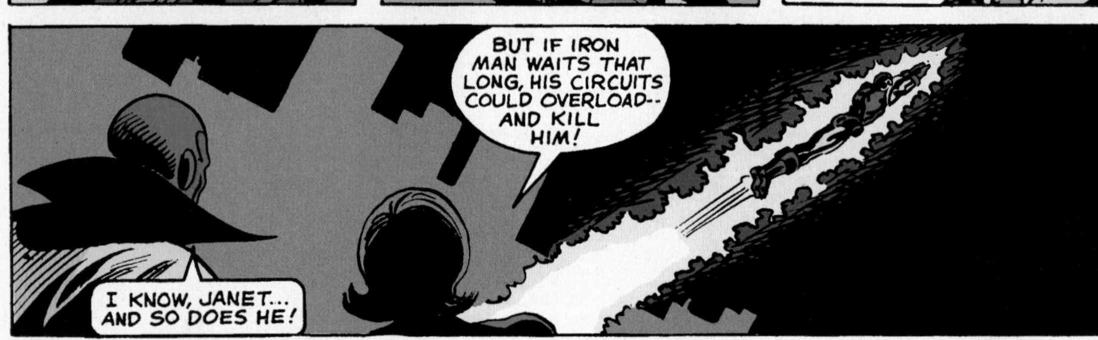
BUT IF IRON MAN WAITS THAT LONG, HIS CIRCUITS COULD OVERLOAD-- AND KILL HIM!
I KNOW, JANET... AND SO DOES HE!

I REALIZE IT'S RISKY HOLDING THE CHARGE THIS LONG--
ESPE-CIALLY SINCE MY ARMOR'S BEEN MAL-FUNCTIONING LATELY ANYWAY!*
*SEE RECENT IS-SUES OF IRON MAN FOR DETAILS--R.

BUT IF I UNLOADED THIS BUILT-UP POWER IN A POPULATED AREA, THE RESULTS COULD BE DIS-ASTROUS! I JUST HOPE I'M HIGH ENOUGH NOW-- BECAUSE IF I HOLD OUT ONE SECOND LONGER, I'M DEAD! GOT... TO...

--RELEASE!
AND FOR THE BRIEFEST OF MOMENTS, FOR THOSE NEW YORKERS SENTIENT ENOUGH TO RAISE THEIR EYES FROM THE GRITTY PAVEMENTS, A NEW STAR BLAZES OVER THE MANHATTAN SKYLINE...

WHILE TEN MINUTES EARLIER, IN THE PORTION OF THAT SKYLINE OCCUPIED BY AVENGERS' MANSION...
CAPTAIN AMERICA'S BEEN GONE TWO HOURS ALREADY!

JUST HOW LONG DOES IT TAKE TO RECRUIT A NEW AVENGER, ANYWAY?
AS LONG AS IT TAKES, SIR.
HMM, VERY SAGACIOUS, JARVIS.

I ONLY MEANT THAT THE AVENGERS DO THINGS IN THEIR OWN WAY, MR. GYRICH. AND IN THEIR OWN TIME.
AT LEAST... THEY USED TO.
WE STILL DO, JARVIS.

WHO-- MASTER CAP!
WELL, IT'S ABOUT TIME. I HAVE SOME FORMS FOR THE FALCON TO FILL OUT.
YASSUH, I SHO'BE GLAD T'DO THAT LI'L THING.
CAREFUL, FALC-- MR. GYRICH MIGHT THINK YOU DON'T LIKE HIM!

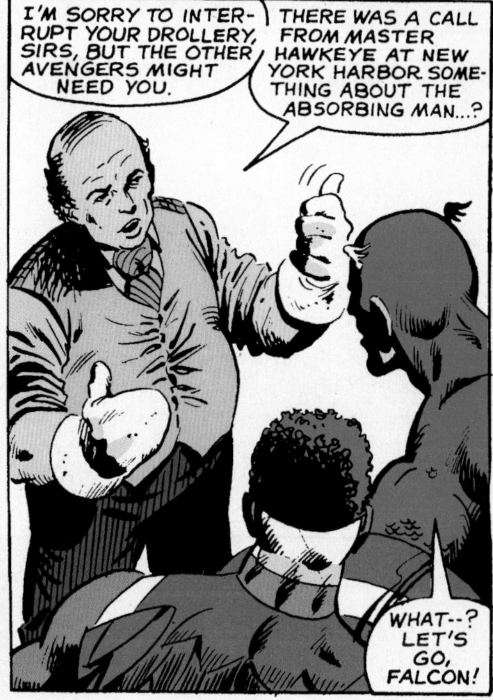
I'M SORRY TO INTERRUPT YOUR DROLLERY, SIRS, BUT THE OTHER AVENGERS MIGHT NEED YOU.
THERE WAS A CALL FROM MASTER HAWKEYE AT NEW YORK HARBOR. SOMETHING ABOUT THE ABSORBING MAN...?
WHAT--? LET'S GO, FALCON!

W-WAITAMIN-IT! WHAT ABOUT PROCEDURES? THE FORMS--?
SORRY, "MASSUH," BUT WHEN CAP GETS A BEE IN HIS BONNET--
--THERE "JUS' AIN'T NO STOPPIN' THAT CHIL'. NOSSUH!"

GEEZ, CAP, THIS BEING A TOKEN'S STARTING TO WEAR PRETTY THIN PRETTY FAST.
I KNOW, SAM--SO FORGET IT!
IF WE'RE GOING TO MAKE THIS PARTNERSHIP WORK, YOU'RE GOING TO HAVE TO ACCEPT A LOT OF THINGS--STARTING NOW.
THERE ARE LIVES AT STAKE.

I, UH, GET THE POINT, CAP. AND I'M SORRY.
COME ON, REDWING. LOOKS LIKE WE'RE AVENGERS NOW!

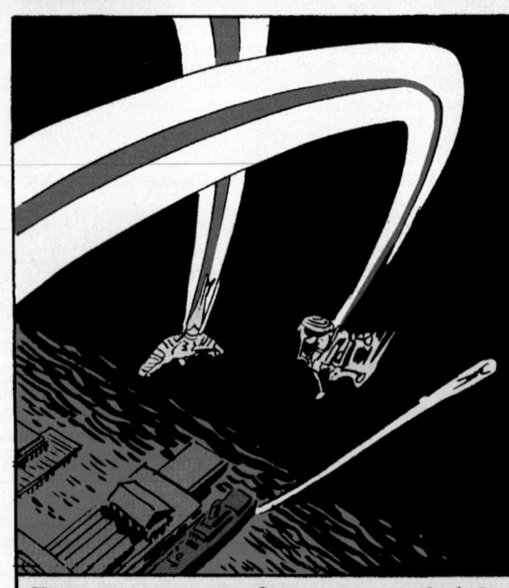

THE JOURNEY VIA SKY-CYCLE AND AIR-FOIL HAD TAKEN EIGHT MINUTES, BRINGING THE TWO HEROES TO THE WEST SIDE DOCKS IN TIME TO SEE AN OMINOUSLY GLOWING IRON MAN STREAKING SKYWARD...

...AND THEN...
YOUR ARRIVAL IS MOST TIMELY, CAPTAIN--AS WILL BE YOUR AID.
HI, FALCON. I LIKE YOUR BIRD!
THAT'S THE GUY WHO'S TAKING MY PLACE IN THE AVENGERS, EH? HE DOESN'T LOOK SO TOUGH TO ME!

SO WHAT'S THE STRATEGY, VISION?
MS. MARVEL AND THE BEAST HAVE TRAPPED THE ABSORBING MAN IN-- MS. MARVEL! WHY AREN'T YOU HELPING THE BEAST?
I WAS GOING TO, VIZH. BUT FRANKLY--

--IT DOESN'T LOOK LIKE HE NEEDS ANY HELP!
WELL, I'LL BE--!

HIYA, GANG! I CALL THIS THE WHIRLY-BIRD--JAIL-BIRD, THAT IS!
AS LONG AS SPONGY CAN'T TOUCH ANYTHING, HE CAN'T ABSORB ANYTHING!
KNUCKLE-HEAD! YOU FORGET I CAN STILL TOUCH--

--YOU!
OOP!

AND YOUR AGILITY, COMBINED WITH MY STRENGTH, SHOULD GET YOU OFF MY BACK FOR GOOD!

DON'T WORRY, BEAST, I'LL TAKE HIM OUT!
CAP! DON'T--!

"UH, CAP?"
"YES, BEAST?"
SKRAKASH
"JUST WHAT IS YOUR SHIELD MADE OF, ANYWAY?"
"A TOP SECRET, SUPER-STRONG ALLOY. WHY?"

JUST CURIOUS. I ALWAYS LIKE TO KNOW--

"--WHAT I'M FIGHTING!"

OH, COME ON! THIS LUG'S TOUGH, BUT HE CAN'T TAKE US ALL ON!
UNWITTINGLY REPEATING WHAT A GROUP OF NOW-BATTERED LONGSHOREMEN HAD SAID EARLIER TODAY,* MS. MARVEL ATTACKS...NOT REALIZING HOW REDUNDANT--AND WRONG--SHE REALLY IS!
*LAST ISSUE, TO BE EXACT--R.

WHILE A SHORT DISTANCE AWAY...
WHAT DO YOU THINK, SIR? SHOULD WE POSTPONE DEPARTURE?
NO, BOSUN. THE DAMAGE IS MOSTLY COSMETIC--

--AND THE ENGINE ROOM TELLS ME THAT EVERYTHING IS STILL FUNCTIONING THERE. PREPARE TO GET UNDERWAY IMMEDIATELY.
I'M BETTING WE CAN STILL REACH PUNTA DEL REY BY TUESDAY.

BUT TO SANDY HERKOWITZ, KIDNAPPED FOR COMPANIONSHIP BY THE ABSORBING MAN ONLY HOURS BEFORE,* THAT'S ONE BET--
POON-TUH-WHO...?
*AGAIN, LAST ISH--R.

--SHE WANTS NO PART OF!
OOOHHH, NO! YOU'RE NOT TAKIN' ME TO ANY JUAN VALDEZ GUEST RANCH--
--WITH OR WITHOUT THAT CREEPO, CREEL!

BUT NOW WHAT? HO-BOKEN, I KNOW--BUT NEW YORK? FORGET IT!
ESPECIALLY WHEN THE ABSORBING MAN COULD BE HULKING AROUND ANY CORNER! IF ONLY--

--WAIT! THAT'S IRON MAN! MAYBE HE CAN HELP ME OUT OF HERE!
OR AT LEAST PROTECT ME FROM THAT SKIN-HEADED FREAK!

BUT AT THIS POINT IN TIME, THE GOLDEN AVENGER HAS OTHER GOALS ON HIS MIND...

...AND OTHER PROBLEMS ON HIS HANDS!
HEY, MAC, DIDN'T ANYONE EVER TELL YOU IT'S NOT NICE TO HIT A LADY?
WHUD
LOOKS LIKE WE'LL HAVE TO TEACH THIS BUM SOME MANNERS, GUYS--THE HARD WAY!

ALLOW ME, GENTLE-MEN!
SHHRAK

I ALMOST FRIED IN THE ENERGY I SIPHONED FROM THIS JOKER--AND THERE'S NOTHING I'D LIKE BETTER THAN TO RETURN SOME OF THAT PAIN PERSONALLY!
THAT'S FINE BY ME, TIN BRITCHES!

LEMME SEE, IRON MAN WAS FLYING IN THIS DIRECTION THE LAST TIME I SPOTTED 'IM.
SO WITH A LITTLE LUCK, HE SHOULD BE SOMEWHERE REAL CLOSE.

INDEED!
FRAKASH
OHNO!

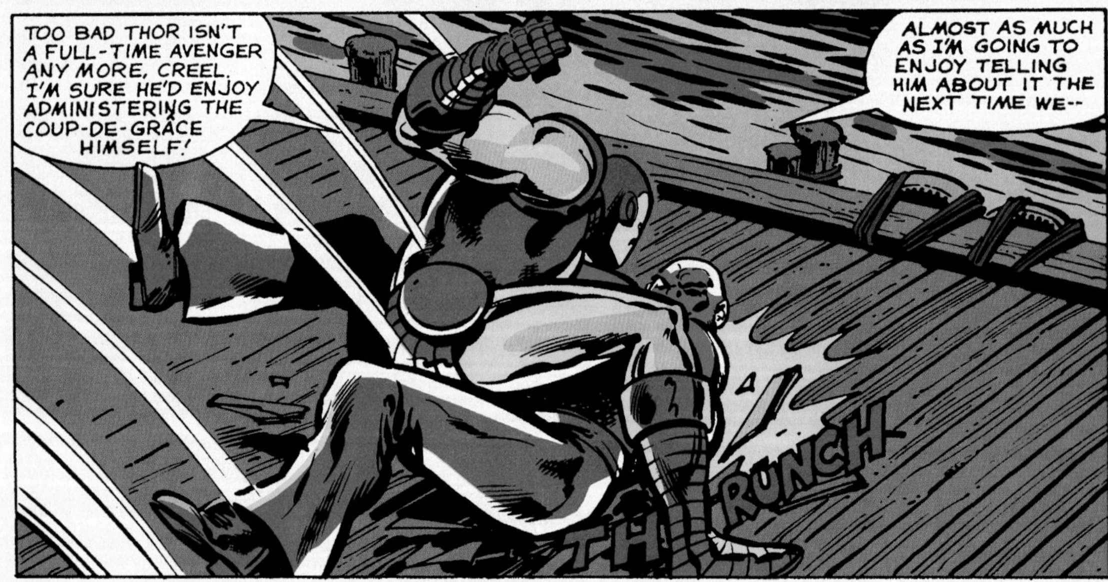
TOO BAD THOR ISN'T A FULL-TIME AVENGER ANY MORE, CREEL. I'M SURE HE'D ENJOY ADMINISTERING THE COUP-DE-GRÂCE HIMSELF!
ALMOST AS MUCH AS I'M GOING TO ENJOY TELLING HIM ABOUT IT THE NEXT TIME WE--
THRUNCH

--HUH?!
I GUESS YA HADN'T NOTICED, HOT STUFF! BUT I'VE ABSORBED THE STRENGTH OF CAPTAIN AMERICA'S SHIELD!
BLANG

AN' THAT MAKES MY BODY AS STRONG AS YOUR ARMOR! OR MAYBE EVEN--
SWOK

KRUNG
--STRONGER!

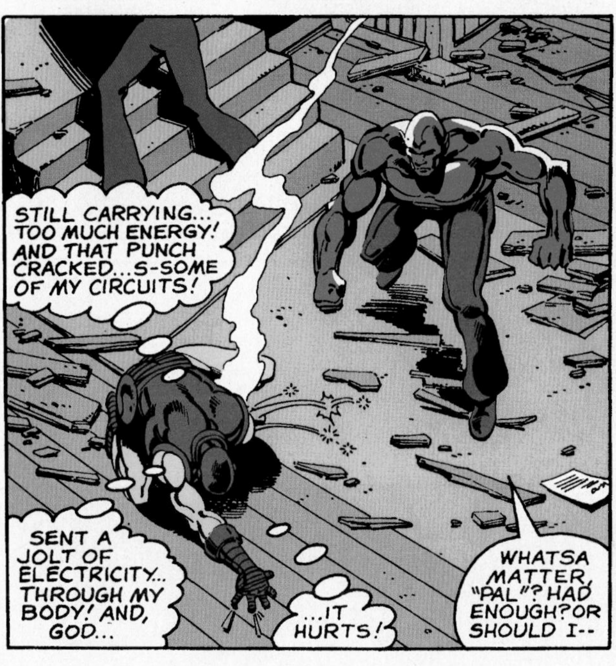
STILL CARRYING... TOO MUCH ENERGY! AND THAT PUNCH CRACKED...S-SOME OF MY CIRCUITS!
SENT A JOLT OF ELECTRICITY... THROUGH MY BODY! AND, GOD...
...IT HURTS!
WHATSA MATTER, "PAL"? HAD ENOUGH? OR SHOULD I--

--HEY, CHIPPIE! I DIDN'T SEE YA THERE!
G-G-GET AWAY FROM ME, YA BIG APE!
YEAH, I MISSED YOU, TOO! LET'S SPLIT!

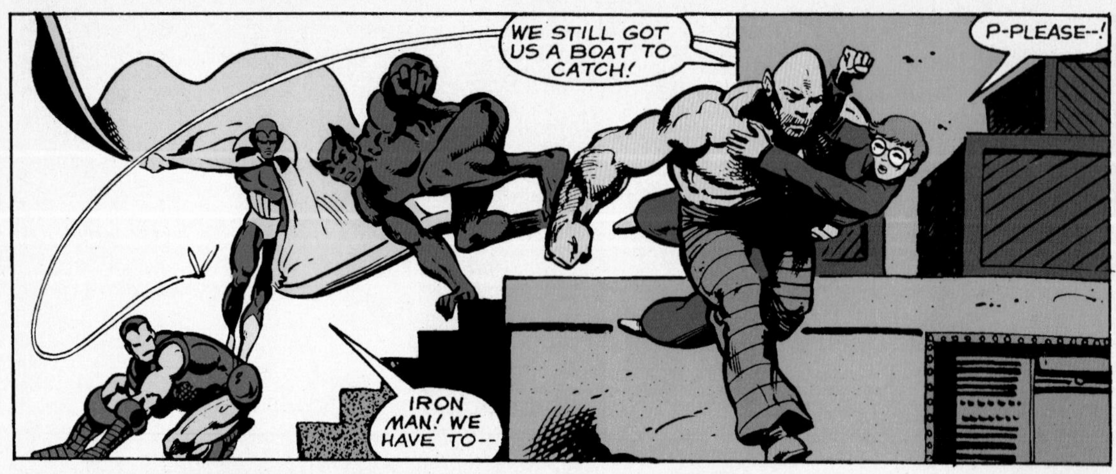
WE STILL GOT US A BOAT TO CATCH!
P-PLEASE--!
IRON MAN! WE HAVE TO--

NOT..."WE", WASP! I'M OUT OF IT! SHOWS WHAT I GET...FOR GOING IT ALONE!
"THE REST OF YOU TRY TO GRAB CREEL! DON'T LET HIM GET AWAY!"

BUT THAT LAST ORDER PROVES SURPRISINGLY UNNECESSARY, AS...
NO! IT CAN'T BE! THIS IS THE RIGHT DOCK, BUT--

--THE BOAT'S GONE! THOSE BLASTED SUPER-HEROES MUSTA DELAYED US PAST SAILIN' TIME!

DAMN THEIR EYES!

WELL, ARE YA HAPPY? ARE YA SATISFIED?
ALL YA HADDA DO WAS LEMME ALONE AN'I'D HAVE BEEN OUTTA YER HAIR FOREVER!
NO, CRUSHER CREEL. THAT WOULD MERELY HAVE BEEN PASSING OUR RESPONSIBILITIES ONTO THE SHOULDERS OF OTHERS. NOW...
...WILL YOU SURRENDER?

YA'D BETTER GET OUTTA THE WAY, CHIPPIE. I GOT A FEELIN' THIS IS GONNA GET MESSY--
--AN' I DON'T WANT YOU GETTIN' HURT.
YOU... YOU DON'T?

C'MON, REDSKIN, I FEEL LIKE SMASHIN' ANYTHING IN A COSTUME!
AN' SINCE YOU'RE THE CLOSEST AT HAND--

--YOU'RE GONNA BE THE FIRST TO FALL!
UNLIKELY. I'M WELL AWARE OF YOUR CAPACITY TO ABSORB MY POWERS, BUT I DON'T THINK YOU'RE AWARE OF THE FULL RANGE OF THOSE POWERS.

FOR EXAMPLE: MY ABILITY TO ALTER DENSITY AT WILL!
HUH? A-ALL OF A SUDDEN... I AIN'T NOTHIN'!
I ALSO DOUBT THAT YOU KNOW HOW--

--TO CONTROL THAT ABILITY!
HEY! I'M FALLIN' THROUGH THE DOCK! GOTTA TURN BACK TO FLESH AND BLOOD--FAST!

AND THOUGH THE ABSORBING MAN SUCCEEDS IN THAT ENDEAVOR--
PLOOOSH
--THE RESULTS ARE LESS THAN GLORIOUS!

THAT'S IT! I CAN'T TAKE THIS NO MORE! THE FIGHTIN' AIN'T BAD, BUT I CAN'T STAND GETTIN' BEAT!
SOMEHOW I GOTTA REACH THAT SHIP!

HOWEVER, A FEW HASTILY SWUM STROKES SOON PROVE TO THE FLEEING VILLAIN--
--THAT HIS NOW-HUMAN ARMS ARE NO MATCH FOR THE MASSIVE TURBINES WHOSE POWER HE SO RECENTLY DUPLICATED.
IT...IT'S TOO FAR AWAY! I-I'LL NEVER MAKE IT! NEVER!

IT IS THEN THAT CRUSHER CREEL GLANCES OVER HIS SHOULDER--
--SEES THREE UNRELENTING HEROES RACING OVER THE OILY WATERS TOWARDS HIM--
--AND REALIZES THAT EVEN HAD HE REACHED HIS GOAL, HE NEVER WOULD HAVE MADE IT.

AND SO WITH A LAST, LINGERING LOOK AT THE DEPARTING FREIGHTER, THE BOBBING SWIMMER CLOSES HIS EYES, HIS FEATURES RELAXING INTO A MASK OF PLACID SORROW--
--AND OF WEARY, WEARY RESIGNATION.

I'VE GOT HIM, AVENGERS! I'LL --EH?!
OMIGOD! HE'S TURNED HIMSELF INTO WATER! DISPERSING INTO THE OCEAN! BUT WHY?!

PERHAPS, MS. MARVEL, THERE IS THAT WITHIN EVEN THE BASEST OF VILLAINS WHICH MAY BE CALLED.... DIGNITY.

AND AS THE THREE PURSUERS RETURN...
SAY, THIS BALL AND CHAIN'LL MAKE A SWELL TROPHY FOR ≥UNF≤...FOR ≥UNG≤...
...SOME-ONE ELSE.
ARE YOU ALL RIGHT, MISS?
HUH? OH, YEAH. I THINK SO. ONLY...
...I THOUGHT THAT GUY WAS A TOTAL PSYCHO.

SO WHY'D HE PUSH ME OUT OF DANGER WHEN HE COULD'VE USED ME AS A HOSTAGE? I MEAN...
...YOU DON'T SUPPOSE IT REALLY WOULD'VE BEEN OKAY TO LET HIM GO, DO YOU?
DO YOU?

NEXT QUICKSILVER AND THE SCARLET WITCH BEGIN A SEARCH FOR THEIR TRUE PAST... THE YESTERDAY QUEST!

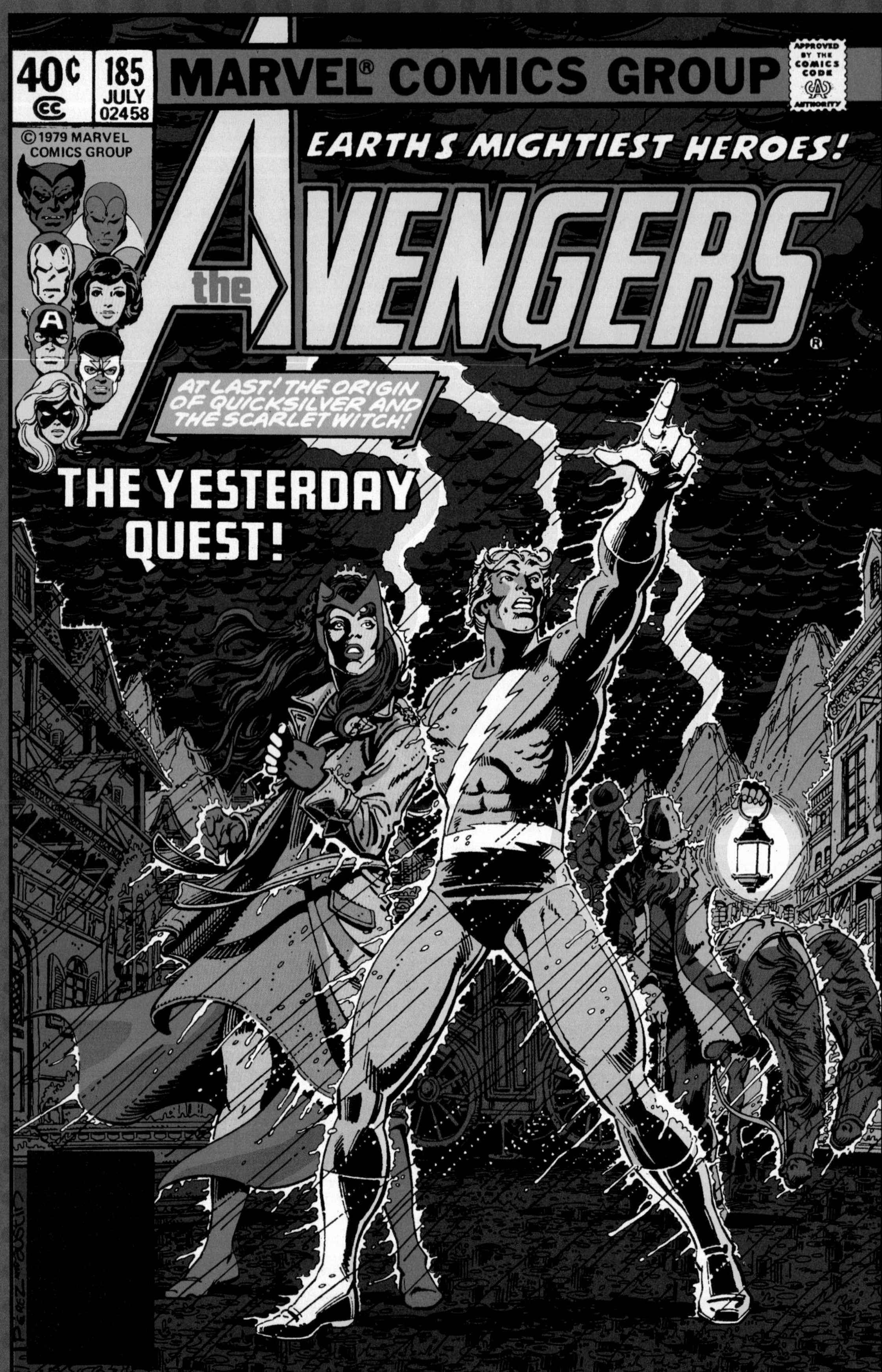
40¢
185
JULY
02458
MARVEL® COMICS GROUP
APPROVED BY THE COMICS CODE AUTHORITY
© 1979 MARVEL COMICS GROUP
EARTH'S MIGHTIEST HEROES!
the AVENGERS
AT LAST! THE ORIGIN OF QUICKSILVER AND THE SCARLET WITCH!
THE YESTERDAY QUEST!

And there came a day when *Earth's mightiest heroes* found themselves *united* against a common threat. On that day, the *Avengers* were born—to fight the foes no *single* super-hero could withstand!

Stan Lee PRESENTS: THE MIGHTY AVENGERS!®

MARK GRUENWALD & STEVEN GRANT PLOT / DAVID MICHELINIE WRITER / JOHN BYRNE PENCILS / DAN GREEN INKS / COSTANZA, letters SLIFER, colors / ROGER STERN, editor / JIM SHOOTER editor-in-chief

THE YESTERDAY QUEST!
EVEN AT THE BEST OF TIMES, NEW YORK HARBOR IS RARELY CONSIDERED TO BE ONE OF THE WORLD CAPITALS OF TIDINESS. AND THIS, QUITE OBVIOUSLY--
--IS ANYTHING BUT THE BEST OF TIMES!
HOLY CRUD, ROSSI! I THOUGHT DISPATCH SAID THERE WAS A "BRAWL" ON PIER 12!
BETTER CHANGE THAT TO "RIOT," SANCHEZ! IT LOOKS LIKE THE AVENGERS HAVE BEEN PLAYIN' BOUNCE-THE-BAD-GUY AGAIN!
AN' I GOT A FEELIN' THE OWNER O' THIS WAREHOUSE AIN'T GONNA BE TOO PLEASED!
N.Y.P.D.
POLICE
NY
LG429

OKAY, IRON MAN, CARE TO EXPLAIN?
OR DO WE JUST SEND THE BILL DIRECTLY TO AVENGERS MANSION?
NOW WAIT A MINUTE! YOU CAN'T BLAME US FOR THIS DESTRUCTION! IT WAS THE ABSORBING MAN! *
*LAST ISSUE--ROG.
OH, YEAH? I DON'T SEE NO ABSORBINE MAN.
BUT HE JUMPED INTO THE HARBOR!
AND THEN HE ABSORBED THE PROPERTIES OF THE WATER AND, UM, DISSIPATED... INTO... AH...
...WOULD A CHECK FROM TONY STARK BE ALL RIGHT, OFFICER?

WELL, REDWING, IT LOOKS LIKE OUR FIRST GIG AS AVENGERS WASN'T EXACTLY FRONT PAGE MATERIAL.
DON'T WORRY, FALCON, YOU MAY NOT HAVE SEEN MUCH ACTION THIS TIME, BUT YOU'LL GET YOUR CHANCE.
"MUCH ACTION"?!

THAT BIRD-MAN DIDN'T EVEN THROW ONE PUNCH!
SO HOWCUM HE'S STILL WITH THE TEAM... AND I'M NOT?

I DIDN'T HAVE TIME TO TELL YOU BEFORE, FOLKS, BUT THE FALCON'S AGREED TO BE AN AVENGER!
THE WOMAN IN BLACK IS MS. MARVEL, FALCON. I THINK YOU KNOW THE REST.
WE'VE MET.
GLADASEEYA, FALC. SAY, HAS ANYONE SEEN HAWKEYE?
NO, BEAST. AND THEY'RE NOT LIKELY TO!

AFTER ALL, WHY SHOULD DEAD WEIGHT HANG AROUND TO CLOG THE WHEELS OF PROGRESS?
LOOK, CLINT--

--THE NEW MEMBERSHIP WASN'T OUR IDEA, AND BEING BITTER ISN'T GOING TO DO ANYONE ANY GOOD.
NO?

JUST WAIT 'LL STARK TAKES AWAY YOUR TIN SUIT AND SENDS YOU OUT TO BE A CIVILIAN, SHELL-HEAD!
THEN YOU CAN TALK TO ME ABOUT BITTER!
THE SILENCE THAT FOLLOWS IS COLDER THAN THE LATE AFTERNOON CHILL, AND GIVES HINT OF A DEADLY DESTINY YET TO COME...

BUT FOR NOW, AT A FAMOUS MIDTOWN MANSION...
I'M SO GLAD YOU'RE BACK, SIRS, MADAMS. MISTER GYRICH WAS MOST DISTRESSED BY--

--EH?! M-MY WORD!
SORRY, JARV! GOT A DATE!
AND THOUGH MELISSA WOULD PROBABLY UNDERSTAND IF I WAS A WEE BIT TARDY--
--JOANIE AND PAM WOULD KILL ME!

I MUST SAY, MASTER BEAST SEEMS TO HAVE OVERCOME HIS FORMER MELANCHOLIA QUITE, UH...
...THOROUGHLY?
INDEED.

AND WE MIGHT AS WELL RELAX, TOO. I HAVE TO GO REPAIR MY ARMOR--
--BUT THERE'S NOTHING ON THE AGENDA FOR THE REST OF US UNTIL MR. STARK DROPS BY TO--

--CHECK ON THE NEW SECURITY SYSTEM. ANY COMPLAINTS, JARVIS?
NONE FROM ME, SIR. THOUGH YOU MIGHT ASK THE OTHERS.

"I THINK I'LL DO JUST THAT," ANSWERS THE YOUNG MILLIONAIRE INVENTOR, TURNING TO WALK A FAMILIAR HALLWAY TO THE MANSION'S SPACIOUS KITCHEN...
THANK YOU, JOCASTA. I LIKE IT BETTER THAN MY OLD COSTUME, TOO. IT WAS DESIGNED BY--

WHOOPS! SORRY, MS. MARVEL. I WAS JUST REACHING FOR THE--
THAT'S OKAY, TONY. YOU CAN BUMP ME ANY TIME.

HMM. IF YOU LIKE MY BUMPS, MS. M., YOU SHOULD TRY MY DIPS.
DO YOU DANCE?
NO. BUT I DON'T SEE WHY THAT SHOULD STOP US...

SMALL TALK... A PASTIME SO INHERENTLY HUMAN. AND FOR THE GLITTERING CYBORG NAMED JOCASTA--
--QUITE FRUSTRATING AS WELL.

FOR SHE FEELS A LONGING, A DESIRE TO JOIN IN THE CASUAL BANTER. AND YET...

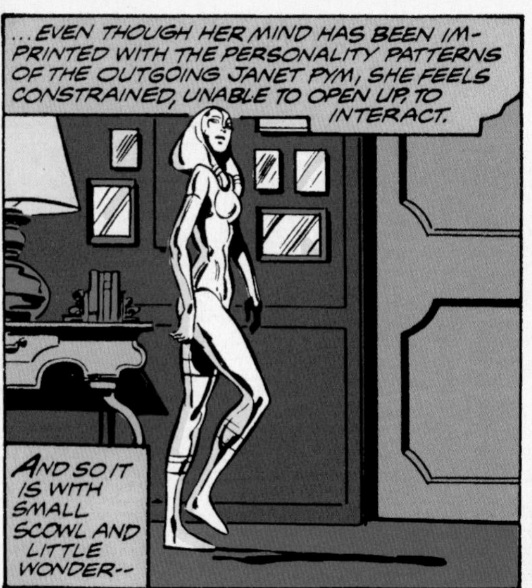
...EVEN THOUGH HER MIND HAS BEEN IMPRINTED WITH THE PERSONALITY PATTERNS OF THE OUTGOING JANET PYM, SHE FEELS CONSTRAINED, UNABLE TO OPEN UP, TO INTERACT.
AND SO IT IS WITH SMALL SCOWL AND LITTLE WONDER--

--THAT SHE SEEKS OUT THE ONE ENTITY WHO MIGHT, IF NOT UNDERSTAND, AT LEAST ACCEPT.
VISION?

AM I DISTURBING YOU?
NOT REALLY, JOCASTA. COME IN.

I JUST THOUGHT YOU MIGHT WANT TO, WELL, TALK.
I'M AFRAID I'VE LITTLE TO TALK ABOUT. I'VE YET TO RECEIVE WORD FROM WANDA AND PIETRO, SO I MUST ASSUME THEIR JOURNEY GOES WELL.
EVEN THOUGH I CAN'T ELUDE A PECULIAR FEELING OF DISQUIET. ONE THAT I DON'T FULLY UNDERSTAND.

BUT THAT'S EASY TO UNDERSTAND, VISION. YOU'RE JUST WORRIED ABOUT YOUR WIFE.
WORRIED? DOUBTFUL. AFTER ALL--

--HOW CAN A MACHINE WORRY?
A... MACHINE?
THE COMMENT CUTS, DEEPLY IF UNINTENTIONALLY. A SITUATION MADE IRONICAL BY THE STATEMENT'S COUNTERPOINT IN FACT.

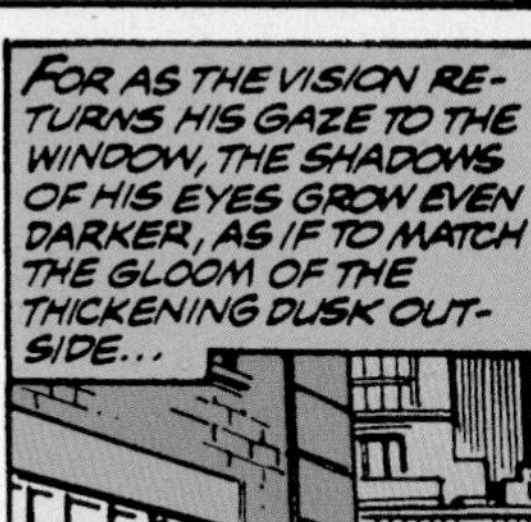
FOR AS THE VISION RETURNS HIS GAZE TO THE WINDOW, THE SHADOWS OF HIS EYES GROW EVEN DARKER, AS IF TO MATCH THE GLOOM OF THE THICKENING DUSK OUTSIDE...

...A GLOOM MIRRORED, SEVERAL DAYS LATER, BY THE GUNMETAL SKIES OF EAST TRANSIA--
--AND BY A LATE WINTER STORM BOTH UNEXPECTED AND, AS SOME OF THE SUPERSTITIOUS VILLAGERS WOULD UNDOUBTEDLY AVOW, NOT WHOLLY NATURAL...

COME, MR. MAXIMOFF, WE HAVE ARRIVED AT THE INN. LET ME HELP YOU.
THANK YOU, MY SON. THE WARMTH WILL FEEL GOOD TO AN OLD MAN'S BONES.

INSIDE...
AH, OUR ILLUSTRIOUS GUESTS HAVE ARRIVED! WUNDERBAR!
YOU RECOGNIZE US?
YA, OF COURSE! THE NAMES OF WANDA AND PIETRO FRANK--THE SCARLET WITCH AND QUICKSILVER--ARE KNOWN TO ALL OF TRANSIA. YOU SHALL HAVE THE BEST ROOMS IN MEIN HOUSE!

AND SO...
REMEMBER, WANDA, SHOULD YOU NEED ME, I AM BUT ONE ROOM AWAY.
I KNOW, PIETRO, BUT I'M NOT WORRIED.
SOMEHOW, I FEEL VERY SAFE HERE. ALMOST AS THOUGH...

...I'VE COME HOME!

LATER...
GOOD NIGHT, MATÉO, MY CHILD. MAY YOUR DREAMS BE FILLED WITH SUGAR PLUMS.
ER, GOOD NIGHT, MR. MAXIMOFF.

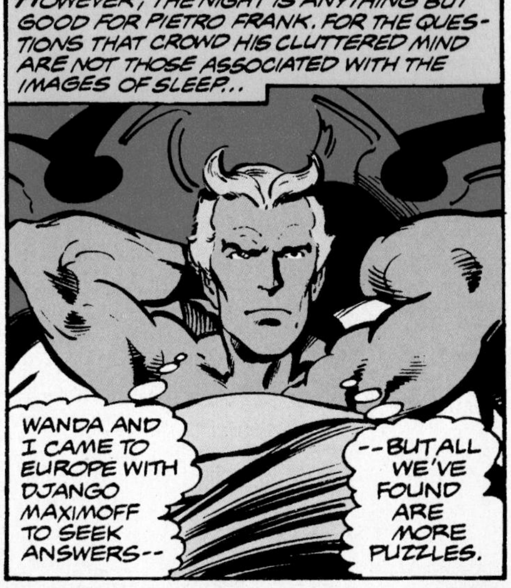
HOWEVER, THE NIGHT IS ANYTHING BUT GOOD FOR PIETRO FRANK. FOR THE QUESTIONS THAT CROWD HIS CLUTTERED MIND ARE NOT THOSE ASSOCIATED WITH THE IMAGES OF SLEEP...
WANDA AND I CAME TO EUROPE WITH DJANGO MAXIMOFF TO SEEK ANSWERS--
--BUT ALL WE'VE FOUND ARE MORE PUZZLES.

FOR SO LONG, WE BELIEVED OUR PARENTS TO BE THE WHIZZER AND MISS AMERICA, AND YET--
--THE OLD MAN'S STORIES RING INEXPLICABLY OF A DIFFERENT PAST!

A PAST LINKED TO THIS VILLAGE--

--AND THAT MOUNTAIN!
BUT HOW? THE MEMORIES ARE SO VAGUE. MY MEMORIES...

"...OF LONG-AGO DAYS IN A WANDERING GYPSY CAMP, OF BEING RAISED BY A KINDLY WOMAN FILLED WITH LOVE, AND A GENTLE MAN WHO CARVED MARIONETTES FOR HIS CHILDREN'S PLAY.
"OH, WHY CAN'T I REMEMBER THEIR FACES?

"I DO RECALL THEIR WORDS, HOWEVER. I RECALL BEING TOLD TO ALWAYS TAKE CARE OF MY SISTER, TO PROTECT HER...

"...AND I RECALL STORIES TOLD 'ROUND A CAMPFIRE, STORIES OF THE GREAT WAR THAT WANDA LATER CAME TO BELIEVE HAD HAPPENED TO HER.
"IT NEVER SEEMED IMPORTANT TO HURT HER WITH CONTRADICTION.

"THOUGH THERE IS PAIN APLENTY IN MY FINAL MEMORY, THAT OF FLEEING FROM THE FLAMING CAMP AS MY FATHER WAS BEATEN BY ATTACKING VILLAGERS-- JUST AS MAXIMOFF DESCRIBED!
"IF THE OLD MAN WASN'T THERE, HOW COULD HE HAVE KNOWN?

"AND WHY DOES WANDA INSIST THAT OUR BIRTHPLACE WAS ON THAT MOUNTAIN, IN THE SEQUESTERED CITADEL CALLED... WUNDAGORE?

"SHE TELLS WITH GREAT SINCERITY OF HOW BOB AND MADELINE FRANK CAME TO THAT LEGENDARY COMPLEX TO HAVE THEIR CHILDREN--

"--OF HOW HEALTHY AND VERY SPECIAL TWINS WERE BIRTHED--
"--AND HOW THE MOTHER DIED TRAGICALLY OF COMPLICATIONS SOON AFTER.

"WE'VE BOTH HEARD SO MANY TIMES THAT THE SKY OVER THE MOUNTAIN WAS FILLED WITH LIGHTS THE NIGHT WE WERE BORN...

"...WHILE TWICE WHEN WANDA'S POWERS EBBED, THEY SEEMED TO BE RESTORED BY RETURNING TO THIS LAND. SO EACH TALE APPEARS TO HAVE A BASIS IN FACT.
"BUT HOW CAN THEY BOTH BE TRUE? HOW?"

NO ANSWER ARISES. NONE WAS REALLY EXPECTED. AND SO THE SILVER-MANED MUTANT CAN MERELY RETURN, FROWNING, TO HIS BED--
--PRETENDING HALF-HEARTEDLY THAT SLEEP WILL SOON COME.

WHILE IN A CHAMBER NEARBY, THE SCARLET WITCH BREATHES SHALLOWLY IN HER WILL-INDUCED SLUMBER...

...A RESPITE THAT IS SOON TO BE SHARPLY, AND EERILY--

--INTERRUPTED!

AWAKEN, MILADY! KNOW THEE THAT I AM *MODRED*, A FELLOW TRAVELLER IN THIS LAND. AND THOU WHO ART DEEMED THE SCARLET WITCH MUST NOW TRAVEL WITH ME--

--IF THOU DOST HOPE TO UNRAVEL THE TWISTED SKEINS OF *TRUTH!*

WH-WHAT?

LOOK, MISTER, I DON'T KNOW WHAT YOU WANT--
--BUT UNLESS YOU FIND A CONVEN-IENT EXIT SOON, I'M GOING TO--
THOU SEEKEST SOLUTIONS TO THE RIDDLES OF THINE PAST, DOST THOU NOT?

H...HOW DID YOU KNOW--?
THAT MATTERS LITTLE.
WHAT DOES MATTER IS THAT I MAY HELP--IF THOU WILST ACCOMPANY ME.

I'LL HAVE TO TALK TO MY BROTHER FIR--OH!
PAF!
NAY! THE PATH WE TRAVEL IS A DANGEROUS ONE, PASSABLE ONLY BY THOSE WELL-VERSED IN THE ARCANE MAGICKS!
MY COSTUME! EVEN I CAN'T DO THAT TRICK!

ALL RIGHT, MODRED. YOU'VE PIQUED MY CURIOSITY. I'LL GO.
THEN JOIN ME IN THE CARRIER NIMBUS, MILADY. FOR TIME IS SHORT, AND WE MUST FLY!

AND THAT, QUITE LITERALLY, IS WHAT THEY DO! LIKE FIREFLY MIST THEY SOAR GENTLY THROUGH THE NOW-DRY SKIES OF TRANSIA...
...ON A JOURNEY THAT DOES NOT GO COMPLETELY UNOBSERVED!

MILES PASS AS SECONDS BENEATH THE SCINTILLATING CARRIER SPHERES--
--MILES THAT AT LAST LEAD TO THE SNOW-SCATTERED, WINDSWEPT FACE OF--

--WUNDAGORE MOUNTAIN! BUT WHY HERE?
THERE ARE REASONS, MILADY. AND TAKE CARE, FOR I SENSE THAT THERE MAY ALSO BE GREAT--

--DANGER!
SOME SORT OF STASIS CANNON! IT MUST BE ONE OF THE HIGH EVOLUTIONARY'S GUARDIAN DEVICES!

BEWARE, MILADY! THE DRAGON DOTH SEEM READY TO STRIIEEEK!
ZZZZHRRK

WHUBUMB
LOOKS LIKE MODRED IS ON THE UP-AND-UP. THAT RAY BLAST WAS MEANT FOR ME!

MAGICIAN! ARE YOU--?
I AM UNHARMED, MILADY. THY MUTANT HEX DID WHAT MINE OWN SORCERY COULD NOT!

BUT NOW WE MUST HASTEN! FOR OUR GOAL RESTS MERE PACES BEYOND THIS RISE.

IT LIES CRADLED IN THE CANYON OF THE HOLLOWED-OUT MOUNTAIN, STILL GLEAMING AFTER SO MANY DESERTED YEARS, A WRECKED RUIN WHOSE PRESENCE SEEMS AS SAD AS IT IS SILENT...

...AS IT IS **AWESOME!**

BEHOLD! THE ONCE-GREAT MAJESTY OF... **WUNDAGORE!**

THE TWO WAYFARERS STAND STARING FOR A MOMENT, UNSPEAKING, AND THEN BEGIN TO PICK THEIR WAY CAREFULLY TOWARDS THE CRUMBLED SPIRES... EVENTUALLY ROUNDING A FINAL CORNER TO DISCOVER--

--AN ALTAR! AND A BOOK FLOATING ABOVE IT! DO YOU HAVE ANY IDEA WHAT IT MEANS, MODRED?

AYE, WANDA FRANK, THAT I DO. THE TOME BELONGS TO HIM WHO I SERVE.
WHILE YON ALTAR, DEAR LADY... I AM AFRAID THAT--

SSHHRAMM
--IS FOR THOU!

THE CRACKLE OF MAGICAL ENERGY ECHOES AMONGST THE BOULDERS, FADING... LEAVING ONLY THE WHISPER OF MOUNTAIN WIND--
--AND A LOW RUMBLE OF LAUGHTER THAT COMES FROM FAR, FAR AWAY...

MORNING.
I HOPE YOU AND ANA PLAN TO HAVE BREAKFAST, MY SON. IT'S A MOST IMPORTANT MEAL, YOU KNOW.
WANDA?
TEP TEP
PERHAPS. SOME PORRIDGE WITH DOLLOPS OF HONEY...?

WE'VE MUCH TO DO TODAY, AND--
--WHAT?! SHE'S GONE!

A-ALL RIGHT, MATÉO, YOU DON'T HAVE TO HAVE PORRIDGE!
SCONES ARE NICE, TOO!

MY SISTER! HAVE YOU SEEN HER?
W-WHY, NO, HERR FRANK! NO ONE HAS GONE IN OR OUT ALL MORNING!

BLAST! TAKE CARE OF MR. MAXIMOFF, WILL YOU? HE'S A LITTLE MAD, BUT HARMLESS.
WELL, UH, I-I SUPPOSE I COULD...
BUT, MATÉO--

--I DON'T WANT TO BE LEFT ALONE...
...AGAIN.

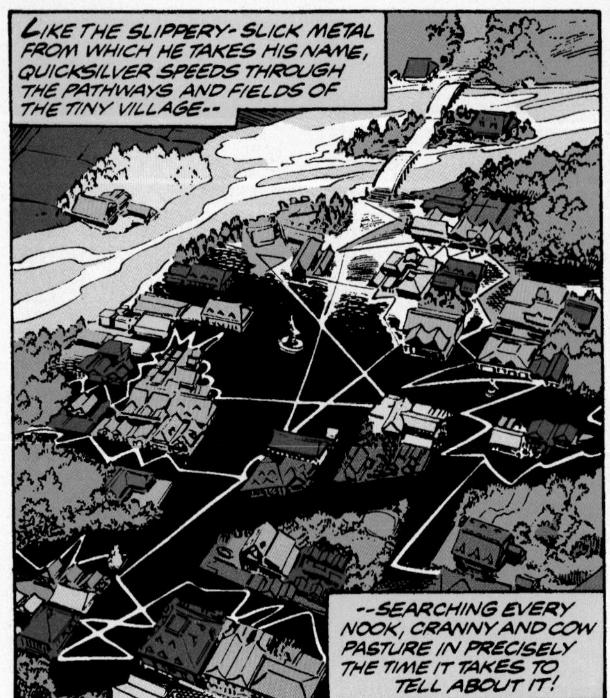
LIKE THE SLIPPERY-SLICK METAL FROM WHICH HE TAKES HIS NAME, QUICKSILVER SPEEDS THROUGH THE PATHWAYS AND FIELDS OF THE TINY VILLAGE--
--SEARCHING EVERY NOOK, CRANNY AND COW PASTURE IN PRECISELY THE TIME IT TAKES TO TELL ABOUT IT!

THOUGH THE RESULTS OF THAT SPECTACULAR SEARCH ARE FAR FROM SATISFYING.
NOTHING! NOT A HINT, A CLUE!
I SHOULD NEVER HAVE LEFT WANDA ALONE!

I COME THOUSANDS OF MILES TO FIND THE TRUTH OF MY FAMILY--
--AND I ONLY SUCCEED IN LOSING MY SISTER!
PARDON, HERR QUICKSILVER, BUT MEIN PAPA SAYS THAT YOU ARE LOOKING FOR FRAÜLEIN FRANK.
I TINK I KNOW WHERE SHE WENT.

EH? WHAT ARE YOU SAYING, GIRL?
I SAW A LIGHT FROM MEIN WINDOW LAST NIGHT. I TINK YOUR SISTER FLEW OFF TO DER MOUNTAIN. IS SHE A FAERIE?

"THEY SAY THERE WERE LIGHTS ON THE MOUNTAIN THE NIGHT WE WERE BORN..."
GOOD GOD!

THANK YOU, CHILD! YOUR HELP HAS BEEN INVALUABLE!

I ONLY PRAY THAT IT'S NOT COME TOO LATE!

DESPERATION RESTORES THE SILVER MUTANT'S STAMINA, BLINDING HIS MIND TO WEARINESS--

--JUST AS IT BLINDS HIS EYES TO THE HEAVILY-CLOAKED FIGURE THAT WATCHES HIS PROGRESS UP WUNDAGORE MOUNTAIN.

FOR PIETRO FRANK SENSES THAT HIS SISTER IS IN DANGER--

--HE HAS A GOOD IDEA OF WHERE SHE MAY BE--

--AND WITH A DETERMINATION INCONCEIVABLE TO MERE HUMANS--

--HE KNOWS THAT NOTHING, BUT NOTHING WILL KEEP HIM FROM HER!

UNFORTUNATELY, HE'S WRONG!
BOMP!
UNGF!
SPOTCH
AND BECAUSE OF THAT ILL-TIMED ERROR--
CHUD
--THE ONLY THING PIETRO FRANK--
SPAK
--KNOWS NOW--
KISH
--IS--
--DARKNESS!
RESTORATION: CONSCIOUSNESS RETURNING IN SLIVERS AND SHADOWS...
UHHNNN. WHAT... WHAT HAPPENED? MY HEAD--!
PLEASE. BE CALM. YOU ARE SAFE, FOR THE PRESENT.

BUT WHO ARE YOU? AND WHERE AM I? HOW DID I GET HERE?
MY, BUT YOU'RE JUST FULL OF QUESTIONS, AREN'T YOU? YOU SHOULD REST, YOU'VE BEEN HURT. I ASSURE YOU THAT ALL WILL BE ANSWERED IN DUE TIME, PIETRO.
YOU... KNOW MY NAME?
OF COURSE. WHO COULD POSSIBLY KNOW IT BETTER--

--THAN THE ONE WHO *BROUGHT* YOU INTO THIS WORLD?

NEXT ISSUE: NIGHTS OF WUNDAGORE!

40¢ 186 AUG 02458

MARVEL® COMICS GROUP

APPROVED BY THE COMICS CODE AUTHORITY

EARTH'S MIGHTIEST HEROES!

the AVENGERS®

THE MOST BIZARRE AVENGERS EPIC EVER TOLD!

ENTER... MODRED THE MYSTIC!

And there came a day when *Earth's mightiest heroes* found themselves *united* against a common threat. On that day, the *Avengers* were born—to fight the foes no *single* super-hero could withstand!

Stan Lee PRESENTS: **THE MIGHTY AVENGERS!**®

MARK GRUENWALD & STEVEN GRANT PLOT / DAVID MICHELINIE WRITER / JOHN BYRNE PENCILS / DAN GREEN INKS / JIM NOVAK LETTERS / ROGER SLIFER COLORS / ROGER STERN EDITOR / JIM SHOOTER EDITOR-IN-CHIEF

HIGH ABOVE THE SUN-STREAKED VILLAGE OF EAST TRANSIA, A TOWERING FINGER OF STONE JUTS SKYWARD.

IT IS CALLED WUNDAGORE, AND IT HAS BECKONED FORTH TWO AVENGERS SEEKING ANSWERS OF THEIR PAST.
ONE, THE SCARLET WITCH REMAINS UN-ACCOUNTED FOR AT ITS PEAK--

--WHILE THE OTHER, QUICK-SILVER, HAS MOST RECENTLY DISCOVERED A LOWER RIDGE, AN UNASSUMING COTTAGE...

...AND THAT COTTAGE'S VERY ASSUMING OCCUPANT.

WH-WHO ARE YOU? WHAT HAVE YOU--?

I'VE PROBABLY SAVED YOUR LIFE, PIETRO. AS THE ONE WHO BROUGHT YOU INTO THIS WORLD, I COULD DO NO LESS!

NOW DRINK THIS MILK SOUP WHILE IT'S HOT. YOU'LL NEED STRENGTH FOR THE TASKS AHEAD.

BUT...

NIGHTS OF WUNDAGORE!

HUSH, CHILD, JUST EAT AND LISTEN. FOR IF ANY OF US ARE TO SURVIVE THIS TIME OF EVIL, YOU MUST KNOW FULLY MY STORY--
--AND YOURS!
"THE TALE BEGINS YEARS AGO, IN THE LABORATORY OF HE WHO WAS TO BE CALLED THE HIGH EVOLUTIONARY. I WAS ONE OF HIS FIRST PROJECTS, A COW WHICH HE EVOLVED TO HUMAN FORM AND NAMED... BOVA!

"I WAS TO CARE FOR THE CHILDREN OF HIS NEW MEN, FOR HE HAD MORE PRESSING MATTERS TO TEND TO. MATTERS THAT COINCIDED WITH THE UNEXPLAINED RETURN OF HIS ASSISTANT, JONATHAN DREW...

"... MATTERS THAT KEPT THE TWO MEN OCCUPIED IN THE TALL TOWERS OF WUNDAGORE THE NIGHT WHEN A VISITOR ARRIVED, ASKING SANCTUARY. HER NAME WAS MAGDA, A WOMAN HEAVY WITH CHILD--
"--AND SORROW...

"SHE TOLD OF A HUSBAND WHO HAD GAINED STRANGE ABILITIES, POWERS THAT HAD SENT HIM RAVING WITH A DESIRE TO RULE THE WORLD. FEARFUL THAT HIS MADNESS WOULD CORRUPT THE CHILD HE WASN'T EVEN AWARE SHE CARRIED, SHE HAD FLED.

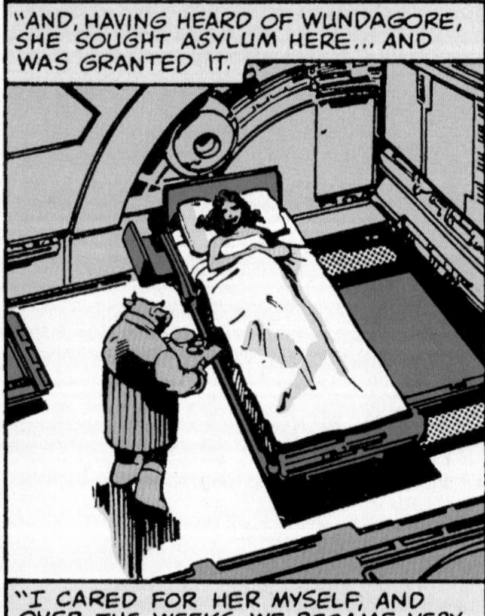
"AND, HAVING HEARD OF WUNDAGORE, SHE SOUGHT ASYLUM HERE... AND WAS GRANTED IT.
"I CARED FOR HER MYSELF, AND OVER THE WEEKS WE BECAME VERY CLOSE.

"SO THAT WHEN THE TIME CAME TO MIDWIFE FOR HER, IT WAS MORE PRIVILEGE THAN DUTY. I HELPED TO DELIVER TWIN INFANTS THAT NIGHT-- YOU, PIETRO, AND YOUR SISTER, WANDA--
"--WHOSE TINY FORM MOMENTARILY MIRRORED THE MYSTERIOUS LIGHTS THAT FILLED THE SKY THE NIGHT YOU WERE BORN...

"MAGDA WAS PLEASED WITH HER OFFSPRING AND YET IT SEEMED A PLEASURE TINGED WITH RESOLVE. THUS IT CAME AS LITTLE SHOCK WHEN, DAYS LATER--

" I FOUND HER GONE, LEAVING ONLY A NOTE EXPRESSING FEAR THAT IF SHE REMAINED ALIVE, HER UNNAMED HUSBAND MIGHT FORCE KNOWLEDGE OF THEIR CHILDREN FROM HER.

"I TOOK THE CHILDREN TO MY LORD HIGH EVOLUTIONARY. HE WAS WEARY, AS IF FROM SOME GREAT CONFLICT, BUT AGREED TO HELP.

"HE THUS SUMMONED A VISITING COUPLE FROM THE VILLAGE BELOW--ROBERT AND MADELINE FRANK, WHO WERE THEMSELVES EXPECTING A CHILD. IT WAS MY LORD'S PLAN TO GIVE ALL THREE CHILDREN TO THE FRANKS.

"AND SO, I PERFORMED ONCE MORE AS MIDWIFE. ONLY THIS TIME THE RESULTS WERE TRAGIC. THE CHILD WAS HORRID, DEFORMED AND, THANKFULLY, STILLBORN.
"THE MOTHER SURVIVED THE RIGORS OF THAT TERRIBLE BIRTH BY ONLY MOMENTS.

"SEEING BUT ONE POSSIBILITY FOR GOOD IN THIS TRAGEDY, I OFFERED MAGDA'S TWINS TO ROBERT FRANK AS HIS OWN. BUT THE DEATH OF HIS WIFE WAS TOO GREAT A BURDEN--

"--AND HE FLED FROM WUNDAGORE, THE SOBS OF HIS GRIEF CRACKING THE CHILL OF THE DARK BALKAN NIGHT...

"IT WAS THEN THAT THE HIGH EVOLUTIONARY TOOK A MORE DIRECT HAND. KNOWING OF A TRIBE OF GYPSIES CAMPED NEARBY, HE ORDERED ME TO FETCH THE CHILDREN...

"...AND THEN, LIKE SOME MANIFESTING GOD, HE PLACED THEM IN THE CARE OF THE TRIBE'S SHAMAN, DJANGO MAXIMOFF, AND HIS WIFE, WITH INSTRUCTIONS TO RAISE THE TWINS AS THEIR OWN.
"THE MAXIMOFFS, WHO HAD RECENTLY LOST THEIR OWN CHILDREN --ANA AND MATÉO-- COMPLIED."

AND THAT'S THE LAST I SAW OF YOU UNTIL YOU CAME TUMBLING DOWN THE MOUNTAIN SOME HOURS AGO.*
THEN DJANGO IS THE MAN WHO RAISED ME IN MY YOUTH! THE STORY FITS! BUT...
*LAST ISSUE -- ROG.

...WHY IS IT SO HARD TO REMEMBER? WHY IS MY CHILDHOOD SO CLOUDY?
PERHAPS IT IS THE TRAUMA OF LOSS, MY DEAR, CAUSED BY YOUR BELIEF THAT YOUR FOSTER PARENTS HAD DIED!

"I FELT THE SAME SENSE OF EMPTINESS WHEN WUNDAGORE LEFT FOR THE STARS, AND I ELECTED TO REMAIN BEHIND FOR... PERSONAL REASONS.
"BUT THAT'S NOT IMPORTANT. WHAT MATTERS IS THAT NOW YOU KNOW ALL."

"ALL"? BUT I STILL HAVEN'T A CLUE AS TO MY TRUE FATHER'S IDENTITY!
THEN TAKE MY WORD THAT YOU KNOW ENOUGH! PLEASE!

THERE IS DANGER HERE THAT SURPASSES YOUR COMPREHENSION, PIETRO!
YOU MUST TAKE WANDA AND LEAVE BEFORE--

WANDA? BUT SHE'S DISAPPEARED! I WAS SEARCHING FOR HER WHEN I FELL!
THEN I'M AFRAID, MY CHILD, THAT IT MUST ALREADY BE--

--TOO LATE? QUITE POSSIBLY. FOR EVEN NOW, AMIDST THE CRATERED RUINS OF WUNDAGORE...

DOTH IT NOT SEEM PASSING DROLL, MILADY, THAT I ONCE CONSIDERED YON TOME, THE *DARKHOLD*, TO BE EVIL?

THAT I EVEN COMBATTED ITS EFFORTS TO HOLD SWAY OVER THE EARTH?

AYE, 'TWAS ONLY WHEN I CONFRONTED ***THE OTHER**** THAT I KNEW THE DEMON OF THE DARKHOLD TO BE AN AGENT OF DESTINY--
--AND THAT 'TWAS MY LOT TO HELP HIM ESTABLISH A NEW ORDER O'ER THE WORLD!
*MARVEL CHILLERS #2-- R.

MODRED DOESN'T REALIZE HE'S BEING USED AS A PAWN!
AND THAT THE ENTITY HE SERVES COULD EASILY ANNIHILATE MANKIND!

NOT THAT HIS OWN POWER IS LACKING. MY MAGIC CAN'T EVEN WEAKEN HIS HOLDING SPELL.

BUT MY MUTANT HEX ABILITIES CAN SIDESTEP MAGIC BY ALTERING PROBABILITIES!
AND, HOPEFULLY, SET... ME...

...FREE!
WHA--? NAY!

FOUL MISCREANT! THOU HAST DEFAMED THE SACRED DARKHOLD!
THAT'S NOTHING, MODRED! AS SOON AS I GET TO MY FEET, I'M GOING TO DESTROY IT!

FIE! MAYHAPS THINE LIFE HATH BEEN DEEMED SACROSANCT BY THE MASTER--
--BUT NAUGHT IN HIS EDICTS FORBIDS THE ADMINISTRATION OF DISCIPLINE!

WRITHE, DEFILER!
WHEW! I BARELY STOPPED MODRED'S MYSTIC BOLTS IN TIME!

BUT I DON'T KNOW HOW LONG I'LL BE ABLE TO HOLD THEM OFF! I THOUGHT MY COMBINED SCIENTIFIC AND SORCEROUS SKILLS WOULD BE A MATCH FOR MODRED--
-- BUT HIS MASTERY OF MAGIC IS INCREDIBLE!

HAVE TO TAKE THE DEFENSIVE! CREATE A HEX SPHERE TO REPULSE HIS ENERGY BOLTS!

THINE RESOURCEFULNESS DOTH BE ADMIRABLE, WOMAN--
--BUT IT SHALL AVAIL THEE NAUGHT!

FOR MINE STRENGTH GOETH BEYOND THAT OF MERE MAGICKS AND SPELLS--
--TO THE RAGING POWER OF THE ELEMENTS THEMSELVES!

A-ALL RIGHT! I BELIEVE YOU! J-JUST STOP! PLEASE--
--STOP!
THOU DOST... YIELD?

VERILY, I BE DISAPPOINTED. I WOULD HAVE THOUGHT THOU TO BE A MORE DETERMINED OPPONENT.
I AM, MODRED. I JUST REALIZED THAT I CAN'T FIGHT YOU ON YOUR LEVEL. BUT THERE ARE OTHER LEVELS. LIKE, FOR INSTANCE, WHAT THE MORTALS OF THIS WORLD CALL--

--A ROUND-HOUSE LEFT!
HNFF?!
THWOK

I... I'VE NEVER KILLED BEFORE! BUT IF THAT MONSTER MODRED SERVES SHOULD PREVAIL, MILLIONS COULD DIE!
GOD FORGIVE ME... !

MAYHAPS "HE" SHALL, WITCH! BUT THE DEMON OF THE DARKHOLD--
SSHHASSH
--SHALL NOT!

FOR THOU WERT CHOSEN AT BIRTH TO BE THE VESSEL, WOMAN! TO BE THE INSTRUMENT FOR THE MASTER'S SECOND RISING! AND THE TIME OF THAT RISING--
--BE NOW!

AND, A SHORT MOMENT AFTER "NOW", ON A FAMILIAR LEDGE
YOU HAVE MY GRATITUDE, BOVA, FOR TENDING MY WOUNDS, REPAIRING MY COSTUME
.AND FOR ARMING ME WITH TRUTH!
BUT I MUST HURRY IN MY SEARCH FOR WANDA, BEFORE-

WAN--
DON'T TROUBLE YOURSELF, BROTHER DEAR! I'VE FOUND YOU!
--DA. ?
OH, MY!

I SHOULD KILL YOU, QUICKSILVER-- AND YOU, COW WOMAN! BUT IT SEEMS I'VE YET TO COMPLETELY CAST OFF MY DAMNABLE HUMAN COMPASSION!

THUS I SHALL LEAVE YOU WITH A WARNING, ONE AS INDISPUTABLE AS IT IS DIRE: GO--

SSHHRAKAMM

--OR DIE!
SH-SHE'S RIGHT, PIETRO! YOU MUST LEAVE!

BUT THAT'S MY SISTER! I DON'T KNOW WHAT'S BEEN DONE TO HER, BUT BY GOD I'LL FIND OUT AND--!
NO! THERE'S NOTHING YOU CAN DO ALONE! IF WANDA OR ANY OF US ARE TO BE SAVED, YOU MUST GET HELP! QUICKLY!

THE ARGUMENT IS SHORT, THE FRUSTRATION IS GREAT... UNTIL AT LAST QUICKSILVER BOWS TO BOVINE LOGIC--

--SKIMMING DOWN THE SIDE OF WUNDAGORE MOUNTAIN LIKE AN EEL ON ICE, AND DARTING INTO THE SURROUNDING FOREST ON A HEADLONG JOURNEY TO--

--THE UNEXPECTED!
MATÉO...?
WHA--? MR. MAXI-- DJANGO! WHAT ARE YOU DOING HERE? THERE IS DANGER--!

OH, FEH! I CAME LOOKING FOR YOU, MY SON, AND DECIDED TO LINGER AWHILE IN THE FOREST.
IT'S SUCH A NICE FOREST, DON'T YOU THINK? WHY, IT WAS HERE THAT I FLED FROM THE NASTY VILLAGERS WHO BURNED OUR CAMP LONG AGO. THIS PLACE HAS ALWAYS MADE ME FEEL SO--

--SAFE...?
THE BRANCHES! THEY'RE ALIVE!

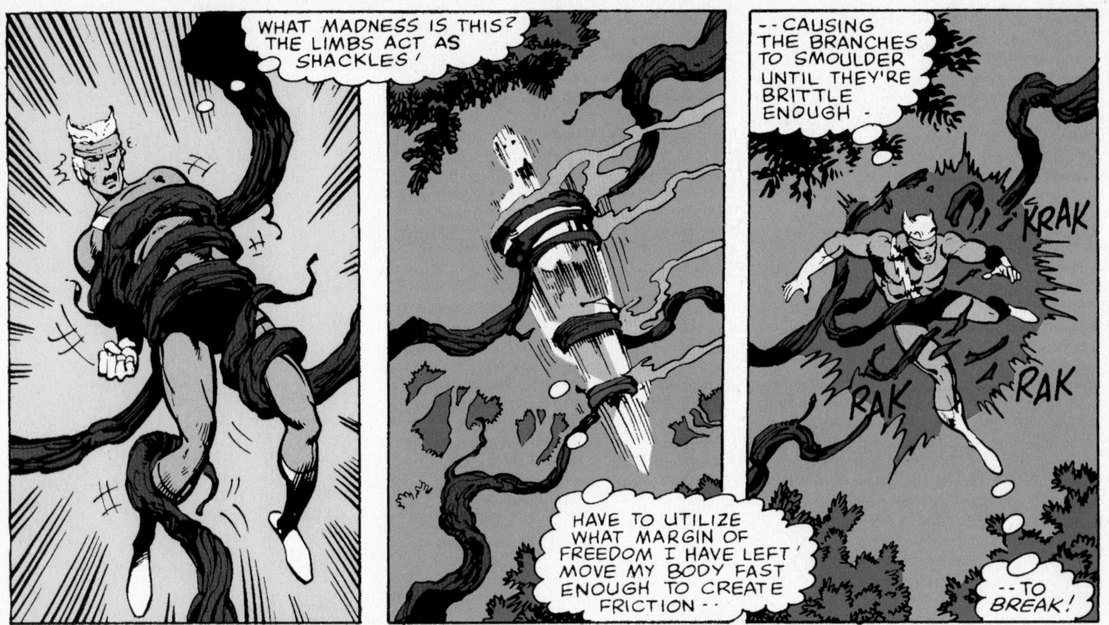
WHAT MADNESS IS THIS? THE LIMBS ACT AS SHACKLES!
HAVE TO UTILIZE WHAT MARGIN OF FREEDOM I HAVE LEFT! MOVE MY BODY FAST ENOUGH TO CREATE FRICTION--
--CAUSING THE BRANCHES TO SMOULDER UNTIL THEY'RE BRITTLE ENOUGH--
KRAK
RAK
RAK
--TO *BREAK!*

DON'T WORRY, DJANGO! I'LL HAVE YOU FREE IN SECONDS!
NO! Y-YOU MUSN'T HARM THE WOOD!

I-IT'S SPECIAL!
AND IT WAS SO FRIENDLY BEFORE I...

I DON'T UNDER-STAND.
I'M SORRY, DJANGO, BUT WE HAVE TO FLEE!

THIS ATTACK WAS LIKELY THE WORK OF AN ARCANE FORCE THAT NOW POSSESSES WANDA! AND I DOUBT IT WILL ALLOW US TO ESCAPE WILLINGLY!

THE AWESOME TRUTH OF THAT STATEMENT IS QUICK TO BE MANIFEST, AS THE ONCE-DRY SKY ERUPTS WITH A STORM AS UNNATURAL AS IT IS IMMEDIATE! AND IT IS ONLY THE INHUMAN SPEED OF THE SILVER AVENGER THAT SAVES THE TWO INNOCENTS FROM A DEADLY RAIN OF FIRE, STONE AND WATER--

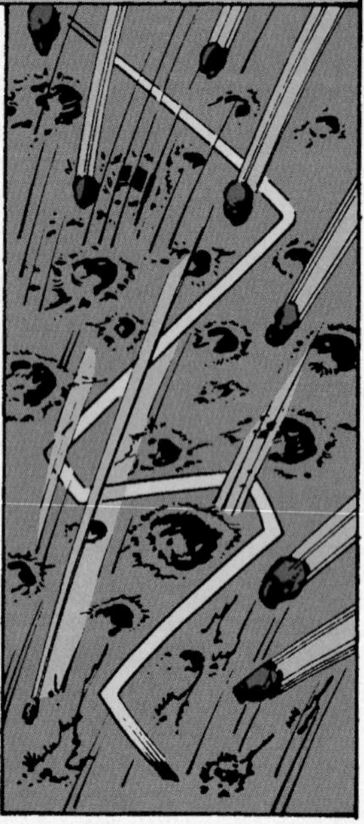

--AS THEY RACE OVER GROUND THAT CRACKS INTO GAPING CHASMS, AS IF THE VERY EARTH WOULD SWALLOW THEM WHOLE!

THAT'S THE POST OFFICE, MATÉO. PERHAPS THEY'LL LET US USE THEIR TELEPHONE. I CERTAINLY HOPE SO.
I-IT'S THE ONLY ONE IN TOWN!

YOU IN THERE! OPEN THE DOOR!
PAMB
PAMB

I AM SORRY, MEIN HERR, BUT WE ARE CLOSED. THE STORM--!
PLEASE! I MUST USE YOUR PHONE! I HAVE TO MAKE AN EMERGENCY CALL TO--

--AVENGERS MANSION, WHERE A SOLEMN, BROODING SYNTHOZOID SITS AT MONITOR DUTY--
--PONDERING THOUGHTS NO HUMAN SAVE ONE COULD PROBABLY FATHOM, THOUGHTS THAT ARE INTERRUPTED BY...
BZZZT BZZZT
THE PRIORITY FREQUENCY!

THE VISION SPEAKING! STATE YOUR IDENTITY, LOCATION AND SITUATION, PLEASE!
THIS IS QUICK-SILVER, ROBOT!

I'M IN TRANSIA, JUST BELOW WUNDAGORE! AND MY SITUATION IS DESPERATE--
--IN THE EXTREME!

WHILE IN ANOTHER PART OF THE MANSION...
FUNNY HOW THE TABLE SEEMS EMPTY WITHOUT OL' SHELL-HEAD AROUND. UH, NOT THAT I HAVE ANYTHING AGAINST YOU, CAP--!
I UNDERSTAND, BEAST. I WAS AS SHOCKED AS ANY-ONE WHEN IRON MAN KILLED THAT CARNELIAN OFFICIAL.*
*SEE IRON MAN #124-125 FOR DETAILS--R.

BUT THE POLICE BELIEVED HIS STORY ABOUT HIS ARMOR ACTING ON ITS OWN, AND SO DO I. MY STINT AS CHAIRMAN WILL BE TEMPORARY AT MOST, AND WHEN THE INVESTIGATION CLEARS IRON MAN--

I'M AFRAID WE CANNOT WAIT THAT LONG, AVENGERS! FOR TWO OF OUR NUMBER ARE IN GRAVE DANGER!
WHAT?
SAY WHO, VISION? SPIT IT OUT, MAN!

QUICKSILVER JUST CALLED, SAYING THAT WANDA HAS BEEN POSSESSED BY SOME PRETERNATURAL POWER--CAUSING HER TO WREAK ELEMENTAL DESTRUCTION OVER AN AREA OF MILES!
ALL RIGHT, GROUP, DOUBLETIME TO THE QUINJET HANGAR! WE'RE ON OUR WAY TO--

I'M SORRY, CAPTAIN AMERICA, BUT YOU'RE NOT GOING ANYWHERE.
GYRICH! WHAT DO YOU MEAN--?

WHAT I MEAN IS: (A) QUICKSILVER IS NOT CURRENTLY AN ACTIVE AVENGER--YOU'RE NOT REQUIRED TO ANSWER HIS SUMMONS.
(B) THERE'S NO PROOF THAT THE MENACE IN BULGARIA IS A THREAT TO U.S. SECURITY, AND (C)--

NOW WAIT JUST A MINUTE--!
--AND (C) ANOTHER INTERNATIONAL INCIDENT WE DON'T NEED!
WE'RE STILL TRYING TO PLACATE RUSSIA OVER THAT SHIELD INVASION LAST MONTH* AND--
*IN IRON MAN #119-120 -- R.

--HEY! WHERE ARE YOU GOING?
TO MAKE A PHONE CALL, MISTER! I'M AS PATRIOTIC AS THE NEXT MAN-- BUT ENOUGH IS ENOUGH!

SAY, GYRICH, HOW'D YOU LIKE TO TAKE A LONG WALK-- ON YOUR FACE?
CUTE, BEAST. NOW, WHY DON'T YOU GO PLAY JOHNNY WEISSMULLER OR SOMETHI--

--EH?
PARDON ME, SIR, BUT THERE'S A CALL FOR YOU. IT APPEARS TO BE URGENT.
BLAST!

LOOK, I GAVE SPECIFIC ORDERS NOT TO BE DISTURBED! JUST WHO THE BLAZES DO YOU THINK YOU--
OH. I-I'M SORRY, SIR, I DIDN'T REALIZE...
...WHAT'S THAT? OH, O-OF COURSE. I'LL TELL THEM.
YES, SIR. GOOD-BYE.
THAT WAS THE :AHEM: COMMANDER-IN-CHIEF. HE'S REQUESTED THAT THE AVENGERS LEAVE ON A, UH, "GOOD-WILL TOUR" OF BULGARIA.
RIGHT AWAY.
YOU CAN WIPE THAT SMIRK OFF YOUR FACE NOW, CAPTAIN.

OKAY, THEN, EVERYONE TO THE HANGAR, ON THE DOUB--.
AH-AH, NOT QUITE EVERYONE, CHAIRMAN.
THE VISION STAYS HERE!

AS PER REGULATIONS, SOMEONE MUST REMAIN ON MONITOR DUTY AT ALL TIMES. AND SINCE THE VISION IS AT THE TOP OF THE DUTY ROSTER--
BUT IT IS MY WIFE WHO IS IN DANGER!
--AH, YES, I REALIZE THAT YOU HAVE A PERSONAL STAKE IN THIS, BUT--

THEN I SUGGEST YOU RECONSIDER, HUMAN!
OR YOU SHALL SEE HOW "PERSONAL" AN ANDROID CAN GET!

NO, VISION! ONE PUNCH COULD CANCEL ALL THE PRIVILEGES WE'VE WORKED SO HARD FOR! WE'LL FIND WANDA AND TAKE CARE OF HER! I PROMISE!
JUST HOLD OFF! WE CAN SETTLE THIS LATER!
FOR A MOMENT, THE VISION SMOULDERS--

--AND THEN, RELUCTANTLY, ACQUIESCES... ANSWERING WITH A TONE THAT WOULD CHILL SNOW.
YES... IT WILL BE SETTLED.

WHILE IN A STORM-WRACKED POST OFFICE SIX TIME-ZONES AWAY...
I'M WORRIED, DJANGO. THE CONNECTION WAS BAD. I'M NOT SURE IF THEY UNDERSTOOD.
I, TOO, AM WORRIED, MY SON. IF ONLY I COULD SEE MY ANA ONCE MORE.

I SERIOUSLY DOUBT, OLD MAN, THAT YOU WILL EVER DO THAT AGAIN.
A...ANA...?

SHRA-
-KOOOM

NO, YOU OLD FOOL! FOR AT LAST I'VE PURGED THIS VESSEL OF ITS LAST TAINT OF HUMANITY, ITS LAST WISP OF SOUL! THERE IS NO ANA MAXIMOFF! THERE IS NO WANDA FRANK! NOW, THERE IS ONLY...
...CHTHON!
NEXT ISSUE: THE CALL OF THE MOUNTAIN THING!

40¢

187
SEPT
02458

MARVEL® COMICS GROUP

APPROVED BY THE COMICS CODE AUTHORITY

EARTH'S MIGHTIEST HEROES!

the AVENGERS®

TM

CAPTAIN AMERICA!
Ms. MARVEL! The FALCON!
QUICKSILVER! The WASP!
WONDER MAN!
ALL AT THE MERCY OF...

THE WITCH ON WUNDAGORE MOUNTAIN!

And there came a day when *Earth's mightiest heroes* found themselves *united* against a common threat. On that day, the *Avengers* were born—to fight the foes no *single* super-hero could withstand!

Stan Lee PRESENTS: THE MIGHTY AVENGERS!®

MARK GRUENWALD & STEVEN GRANT PLOT / DAVID MICHELINIE WRITER / JOHN BYRNE PENCILS / DAN GREEN INKS / JIM NOVAK LETTERS / GEORGE ROUSSOS COLORS / ROGER STERN EDITOR / JIM SHOOTER EDITOR-IN-CHIEF

PORTRAIT OF A TRAVEL AGENT'S NIGHTMARE: THE NORMALLY SERENE AND SCENIC VILLAGE OF TRANSIA, COUCHED IN THE FAIRYTALE VALLEY BELOW WUNDAGORE MOUNTAIN, HAS SUDDENLY BECOME A BATTLEGROUND FOR THE ELEMENTS!

AND CAUGHT IN THAT METEOROLOGICAL HOLOCAUST: SIX MEMBERS OF THE VALIANT, DARING AND, QUITE POSSIBLY, SOON TO BE *LATE* AVENGERS!

THAT'S THREE ENGINES GONE, CAP! AND THE DIALS ARE DOING FLIPFLOPS! I DON'T KNOW HOW MUCH LONGER I CAN KEEP US IN THE AIR!

A3701

THE CALL OF THE MOUNTAIN THING!

LG487

BLAST! I'M SORRY I GOT YOU INTO THIS, WONDER MAN. BUT WITH IRON MAN ON ENFORCED LEAVE...*
DON'T APOLOGIZE, CAP. I'M GLAD TO BE BACK.
AND FROM WHAT YOU SAY ABOUT THAT MESSAGE YOU GOT FROM QUICKSILVER BEFORE HE AND WANDA DISAPPEARED**, WE'RE GOING TO NEED ALL THE "MUSCLE" WE CAN GET!
*SEE RECENT ISSUES OF IRON MAN. **LAST ISSUE--ROG.

MAYBE. BUT IT'LL TAKE MORE THAN MUSCLE TO SAVE THIS SHIP. EVERYONE WHO FLIES, GRAB SOMEONE WHO DOESN'T--WE'RE BAILING OUT!
SORRY, CAP, I'M STAYING. SOMEONE HAS TO MAKE SURE THIS CRATE DOESN'T LAND ON ANYTHING LIVING!

NEGATIVE, BEAST. YOUR CONCERN IS COMMENDABLE, BUT I CAN'T ALLOW--
LISTEN, CAP, I'M NEARLY INDESTRUCTIBLE, REMEMBER? SO WHY DON'T YOU GUYS JUST GO ON--

"--I'LL HANDLE THINGS HERE."

THANKS FOR OFFERING, WONDY, BUT I CAN--HUH?! WH-WHAT'RE YOU DOING--?

I'M STRAPPING ON MY SHORT-RANGE ROCKET BELT, BEAST!
WHEN I SAY I'LL HANDLE SOMETHING, I MEAN--

--I'LL HANDLE IT!
ULP! SO I SEE!

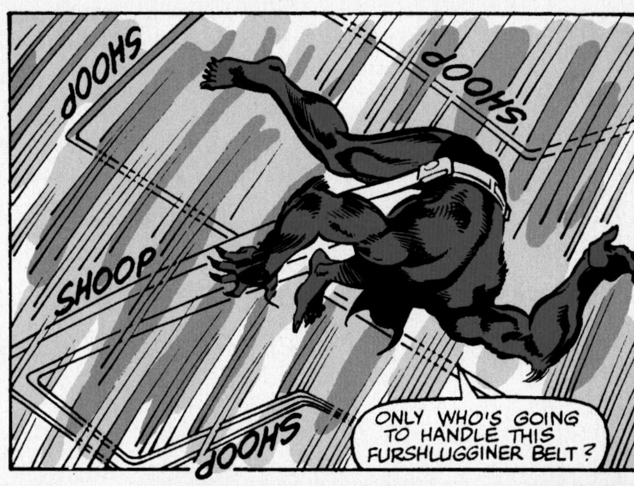
SHOOP
SHOOP
SHOOP
SHOOP
ONLY WHO'S GOING TO HANDLE THIS FURSHLUGGINER BELT?

WHILE BACK IN THE BUCKING COCKPIT OF THE DISABLED AIRCRAFT, SIMON WILLIAMS IS HAVING SECOND THOUGHTS ABOUT HIS IMPULSIVE ACT OF HEROISM.
FOR THE CASCADING QUINJET HAS NOW LOST ALL POWER, AND EVEN WITH HIS GREAT STRENGTH, WONDER MAN HAS DIFFICULTY MAINTAINING CONTROL.

HE FIGHTS, STRAINS, CRIES OUT IN FRUSTRATION...
SKISH
...UNTIL AT LONG, PAINFUL LAST, THE DIFFICULT BECOMES--

--THE IMPOSSIBLE!
FWAWHOOMP
OH, MY GOD!

CAP, YOU WANT ME TO CHECK--?
NO, FALCON, WE'LL NEED YOU HERE. WONDER MAN SAID HE WAS INDESTRUCTIBLE--
--AND ALL WE CAN DO IS PRAY THAT HE WAS RIGHT...!

MEANWHILE, OUR MAIN OBJECTIVE IS THAT VILLAGE, THE MOST LIKELY PLACE FOR QUICKSILVER TO HAVE MADE HIS CALL.
SO WE'D BETTER MAKE TRACKS. WANDA AND PIETRO ARE COUNTING ON OUR--

--HHHEE-EELLP!
YOUR CONCERNS ARE MOST NOBLE, WARRIOR! BUT THY FRIENDS LIE FAR BEYOND THE REACH OF THINE AID!
SSZZZZAK
WHO--?

I AM MODRED, AND I HAVE COME TO FETCH THEE AS DISCIPLES OF THE ONE GREAT LORD--
--CHTHON!

YOU TALK IT UP BIG, MISTER! BUT I'VE GOT A COUPLE OF BIG WORDS MY-SELF! LIKE--
--AVENGERS ASSEMBLE!

WHA--? HOLY CRUD! JUST WHEN IT FINALLY STOPS RAININ', THIS DUDE CONJURES UP A SHOWER OF ROCKS!
DON'T TALK ABOUT IT, FALCON. JUST DO YOUR JOB!

SWELL. FOR A MINUTE THERE, I FORGOT I WAS THE NEW KID ON THE BLOCK.

BUT MAYBE I CAN MAKE AN IMPRESSION ON THESE HIGH-AND-MIGHTY AVENGERS--
--BY LAYIN' IN THE FIRST PUNCH!
THOU... DAREST TO LAY HANDS UPON AN EMISSARY OF THE GREAT LORD?!
FWOK

BLASPHEMER!
HUH? LEAVES! WHIPPIN' UP ALL AROUND ME!

THY BIRD-LIKE FREEDOM HATH MADE THEE VAIN! THUS, TO LEARN HUMILITY, THOU SHALT FLY NO MORE!
FUMP

AND, SPEAKING OF FLYING NO MORE...
SPLUTCH

OOOOO. I FEEL LIKE I'VE JUST MADE A THREE POINT LANDING-- AND I'VE ONLY GOT TWO POINTS! THAT-- EH? SOMETHING SHINY!
COULDN'T BE PART OF THE QUINJET. MAYBE--

--OH, MY STARS AND GARTERS!

THIS SKULL LOOKS LIKE IT CAME FROM SOME KIND OF ANIMAL. BUT WHAT ANIMAL WEARS ARMOR?

PUZZLEMENT GROWS, AS BENEATH THE OVERCAST, GRUMBLING SKIES OF TRANSIA, THE SOLEMN BEAST CONTEMPLATES, SEARCHING FOR A MEMORY...

...WHILE A SHORT MILE DOWN THE MOUNTAINSIDE HIS COMRADES CONTINUE THEIR SOMEWHAT MORE STRENUOUS ACTIVITY!
THOU ART QUITE DEFT AT AVOIDING YON STONY MISSILES, MILADY!

PRITHEE, LET US SEE IF THOU ART EQUALLY ADEPT--

"--AT SHUNNING THE VERY FIRE OF HEAVEN ITSELF!"
UUHHNNN
SHHRASH

THIS GUY DOWNED FALC AND MS. MARVEL LIKE THEY WERE AMATEURS-- BUT HE'S UP AGAINST AN OLD WAR-HORSE NOW!
ONE WHO KNOWS THAT A LITTLE GUILE CAN OFTEN SUCCEED WHERE A FRONTAL ATTACK--

"--FAILS."
YET ANOTHER WORTHY ATTEMPT, WARRIOR. THOUGH AS THOU CANST SEE, IN THIS WOOD--
SNEK
--ALL LIFE BELONGS TO CHTHON!

GUESS AGAIN, MODRED! MY LIFE BELONGS TO ME! AND YOURS WILL SOON BELONG TO A WARDEN!
OOF!

FOOL OF A FOOL! HOW CANST THOU E'EN HOPE FOR VICTORY O'ER ONE WHO DOTH CONTROL THE VERY ELEMENTS?
WIND! L-LIKE A HURRICANE! CREATING A VACUUM! CAN'T GASP BREATHE! C-CAN'T... BREA... EA...

MEANWHILE, ON THE OTHER SIDE OF THE MOUNTAIN...
WUNNERFUL.

I'M GLAD NO ONE FROM THE F.A.A. SAW THAT LANDING. THEY'D PROBABLY TAKE AWAY MY LICENSE. IF I HAD ONE.
AT LEAST I'M STILL IN ONE PIECE.

ER, THEN AGAIN... MAYBE I HIT MY HEAD IN THE CRASH, BECAUSE NOW I'M SEEING THINGS!
LIKE A BIG BALL OF FLYING LIGHT THAT LOOKS JUST LIKE--

--WANDA?!
NO, MORTAL--

--NOT ANY MORE!
SOME SORT OF ENERGY, SHEATHING ME! CARRYING ME OFF LIKE I DIDN'T WEIGH AN OUNCE! AND I...
...I CAN'T LIFT A FINGER TO STOP IT!

WHILE, CONTEMPORANEOUSLY, BACK AT THE SCENE OF THE FALLEN AVENGERS...
VERILY, IF THESE BE EXAMPLES OF WHAT MORTAL MIGHT HATH COME TO, CHTHON SHALL HAVE LITTLE HINDRANCE IN ESTABLISHING HIS NEW ORDER.

YOU'D BETTER TELL "CHIFFON" TO MAKE PART OF THAT ORDER A MEMORY COURSE, WHITE-EYES! 'CAUSE IN CASE YOU HAVEN'T NOTICED--
FSSZAK

--YOU FORGOT THE WINSOME WASP!

ALAS, MY DEAR, THAT HE DID. BUT I--
SSHHHRAPP

-- DID NOT!
CURLS OF ARCANE FORCE STREAM FROM A HAND THAT ONCE BELONGED TO WANDA FRANK--
--AND FOUR SEMI-CONSCIOUS AVENGERS FIND THEMSELVES WAFTED, LIKE SUMMER LEAVES, THROUGH FOREST AND GLADE--
--UP THE SIDE OF WUNDAGORE MOUNTAIN--

--AND INTO A SCENE OF FROZEN HELL!

IT IS DONE--THE CIRCLE IS COMPLETE. SOON, BY THE POWER OF THE DARKHOLD, THIS WORLD SHALL BE MINE--OR ELSE LIE DECIMATED, A BLOOD-SPATTERED SMEAR BENEATH MY THUMB!

THIS MOMENT HAS BEEN A LONG TIME COMING, MODRED, AND I HAVE WAITED FOR IT, PATIENTLY...

.. EVER SINCE THE DAY, EONS AGO, WHEN I FIRST SCRIBED THE DARKHOLD IN WORDS OF FIRE. MY SISTER AND I WERE THE LAST OF THE EARTH-SPIRITS WHO FORMED THIS FERTILE SPHERE, YET WE WERE TO BE DEPOSED BY NEWER GODS. HOWEVER, EVEN SPIRITS SHUN DEATH--
"--AND SO MY SISTER INFUSED HER ESSENCE INTO ALL LIVING THINGS, SURVIVING IN LEGEND AS MOTHER EARTH--
"--WHILE I FLED TO A NETHER PLANE, LEAVING THE DARKHOLD TO PROVIDE A GATEWAY FOR MY EVENTUAL RETURN.

"THROUGH THE YEARS, MY INDE-STRUCTABLE TOME ENDURED, BEING USED AND MISUSED BY MYSTICS AND DABBLERS OF MANY NATIONS WHILE, PATIENTLY, I BIDED MY TIME.

"THEN, IN THE DARK AGES OF THE SIXTH CENTURY, THE BEGUILING MORGAN LE FEY AND HER CULT OF SELF-STYLED DARKHOLDERS SOUGHT TO SUMMON ME TO SERVE THEM.

"BUT I AM BEYOND THE CONTROL OF ANY FOOLISH MORTAL, AND WHEN THE DARKHOLDERS LEARNED THEIR ERROR, THEY TRIED TO BANISH ME BACK TO THE NETHER-REALM--
"--BUT WERE SUCCESSFUL ONLY IN IMPRISONING ME IN THE MOUNTAIN THAT WAS LATER TO BE CALLED WUNDAGORE

"IT WAS AT THIS TIME THAT A TRAITOR IN MORGAN'S BAND--ONE MAGNUS BY NAME--STOLE THE DARKHOLD AND SECRETED IT IN AN ENCHANTED TOWER WHERE NO ONE WITH EVIL INTENT COULD ENTER...

"... BUT EVEN THERE, THE DARKHOLD WAS NOT WITHOUT POWER. FOR THE WELL-MEANING MODRED SOUGHT TO USE THE TOME FOR GOOD--
"--AND PAID FOR THAT FOLLY WITH HIS SOUL!

"THE DARKHOLD WAS LATER REMOVED BY ST. BRENDAN, AND PASSED THROUGH HISTORY IN THE HANDS OF MANY LEARNED AND UNLEARNED MEN: CAGLIOSTRO, TABOO--
"--AND FINALLY GREGOR RUSSOFF, WHO CURSED HIS OWN NAME WITH ITS EVIL.

"TO FINANCE HIS DARK PURSUITS, RUSSOFF SOLD PART OF HIS ESTATE, WHICH INCLUDED THE MOUNTAIN IN WHICH I WAS IMPRISONED.
"THE SCIENTIST BUYERS FOUND URANIUM THERE, AND USED THAT WEALTH TO BUILD WUNDAGORE.

"I PUZZLED AT THE STRANGE MAGIC CALLED 'SCIENCE' THAT TURNED ANIMALS INTO MEN ABOVE ME, AND FOR A TIME CONSIDERED USING THESE NEW MEN AS MY PAWNS--

"--BUT MORGAN LE FEY'S RENEGADE FOLLOWER HAD SOMEHOW TAKEN THE FORM OF THE HIGH EVOLUTIONARY'S COLLEAGUE, INSTILLING THE NEW MEN WITH A SENSE OF CHIVALRY THAT RENDERED THEM UNSUITABLE.

"FORCED TO RELY SOLELY ON MY FEARSOME HOST, THE OTHER, I ATTACKED WUNDAGORE ALONE--
"--ONLY TO BE VANQUISHED BY THE COMBINED MIGHT OF SIXTH CENTURY SORCERY AND TWENTIETH CENTURY SCIENCE.

"BUT EVEN IN DEFEAT, I PLANTED SEEDS OF FUTURE VICTORY...
"...FOR A CHILD WAS BORN THAT NIGHT IN WUNDAGORE, A GIRL NAMED WANDA WHOSE LATENT SCIENCE-SPAWNED POWER WAS AWESOME. AS I RETURNED TO THE MOUNTAIN, I IMBUED HER WITH LATENT MAGICAL POTENTIAL AS WELL!

"SEVERAL TIMES AS SHE GREW, I DIMINISHED THE FEMALE'S SCIENCE-ROOTED POWERS, HOPING THAT SHE WOULD TURN TO SORCEROUS ALTERNATIVES. BUT IT WAS ONLY WHEN HER OVERLY PROTECTIVE BROTHER LEFT TO WED THAT SHE SOUGHT TUTELAGE IN THAT AREA--
"--AND AT LAST BECAME THE ADEPT WORTHY OF BEING MY NEW, DUAL-NATURED HOST!

"THERE WAS BUT ONE LAST DETAIL TO BE SEEN TO--THE RENEGADE DARKHOLDER, MAGNUS.
"I KNEW THAT THE RECENTLY REVIVED SORCERER, MODRED, HAD ALREADY BEEN TAINTED BY THE DARKHOLD--

"...AND SO IT WAS A SIMPLE MATTER TO GAIN HIS FULL ALLEGIANCE IN A CONTRIVED BATTLE WITH THE OTHER.
"AFTERWARDS, HE WAS QUITE AGREEABLE TO TRICKING MAGNUS INTO BEING HALF A WORLD AWAY WHEN I AROSE."

AND NOW I HAVE COMPLETELY SUBJUGATED THE SOUL OF WANDA FRANK. HER BODY, HER SCIENTIFIC AND SORCEROUS ABILITIES BELONG ONLY TO CHTHON! AND WITH THEM, I SHALL BEND ALL OF NATURE TO MY WILL! AND--
MY LORD! SOMETHING APPROACHETH!

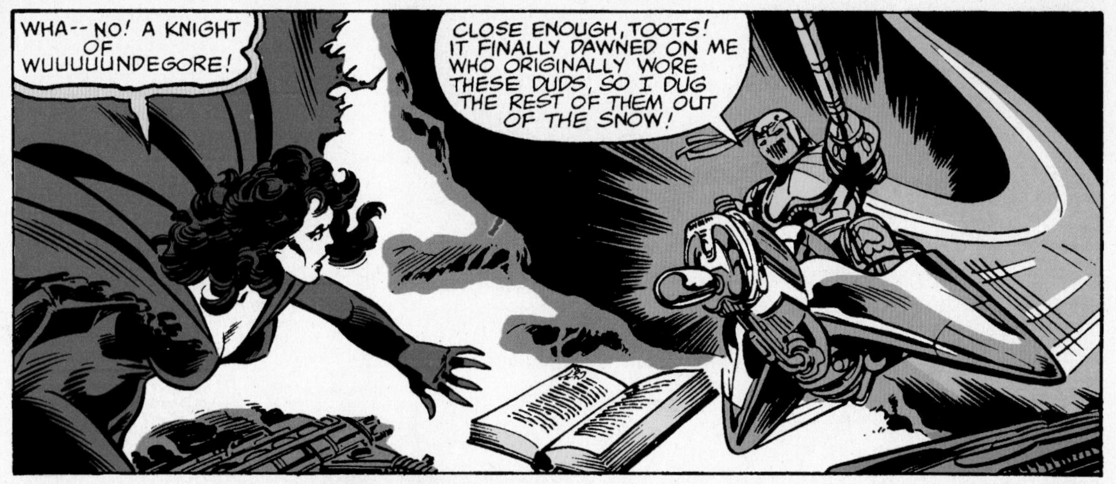
WHA--NO! A KNIGHT OF WUUUUUNDEGORE!
CLOSE ENOUGH, TOOTS! IT FINALLY DAWNED ON ME WHO ORIGINALLY WORE THESE DUDS, SO I DUG THE REST OF THEM OUT OF THE SNOW!

AND JUDGING FROM THAT FAIRY TALE I JUST HEARD YOU SPIN, THEY'RE GOING TO COME IN PRETTY HANDY!
TOUCHÉ!
PRATTLING CUR! THOU SHALT PAY FOR THY FOOLERY WITH THY MORTAL S--
PUTCH

--SSLLGHK?!
SHUK

NICE GOIN', BEAST! YOUR FLASHY ENTRANCE DISTRACTED CHTHON. WE'RE FREE!
YOU TRIIIIICKED ME! FOR THAT, YOU SHALL--

WE SHALL DO NOTHING BUT PUNISH YOU, MON-STER! PUNISH YOU FOR DESPOILING THE BODY OF MY SISTER!
BOOK

YESSSSS! HURT MEEEEE! IT WILL ONLY MAKE THE PAAAAAIN OF YOUR CHASTISEMENT THAT MUCH SWEEEEETER!

OH, ANA, MY CHILD. I WANT SO MUCH TO HELP YOU.
BUT WHAT CAN AN OLD MAN DO? ALREADY, MY HEART RACES LIKE A BIRD'S. HOW--

--EH? THE DOLL! THE ONE IN WHICH I TRAPPED ANA'S SOUL BEFORE! *

IF ONLY THE NIVASHI TALISMAN HADN'T BEEN DESTROYED! I COULD WILL ANA TO COME BACK TO ME... TO COME BACK... COME...

*IN AVENGERS #181-182 -- R.

PAPA?
...BACK...?

MATÉO! Y-YOUR SISTER! THE DOLL--!
--MY HEART...!
WANDA'S SOUL--IN THE DOLL?! THEN THE OLD MAN'S POWER DIDN'T COME FROM HIS TALISMAN, BUT FROM THE DOLL ITSELF!
GOOD LORD! MAXIMOFF SAID HE CARVED THE DOLLS FROM THE WOOD OF WUNDAGORE. THAT WOOD WAS EXPOSED TO THE URANIUM IN THE MOUNTAIN--AND TO CHTHON'S MAGIC! THE POWER IS IN THE WOOD!

BUT HE ALSO SAID THAT OTHERS HAD USED HIS DOLLS*-- I PRAY THIS ONE WILL WORK FOR ME!
WITH ALL HIS WILL, PIETRO STRAINS TO EXCHANGE HIS SISTER'S SOUL FOR CHTHON'S...
*AVENGERS #182--R.

HOWEVER...
DAMN! IT'S NOT WORKING! NOTHING IS HAPPENING!
OF COOOOOOURSE NOT, MORTAL! YOUR WILL IS TOO WEEEEEAK! BUT I DON'T MIND--

--WEAK SOULS TASTE LOOOOOVELY!

I... I'M SORRY, WANDA. I'VE FAILED YOU.
NO, PIETRO--

--NONE OF US ARE MAGICIANS. OUR MINDS WEREN'T TRAINED FOR THIS. NO ONE OF US COULD STAND UP TO CHTHON ALONE.
MS. MARVEL'S RIGHT. OUR ONLY CHANCE IS TO WORK TOGETHER. JOIN HANDS, AVENGERS.

AND THUS ENSUES A LITERAL BATTLE OF WILLS, AS SIX STRUGGLING HEROES POOL THEIR CONCENTRATION INTO A PHALANX OF SORCEROUS THOUGHT, HOPING TO RESTORE A SOUL--
--AND IN THE PROCESS, SAVE A WORLD!

ON THE RECEIVING END OF THAT EMOTIONAL BARRAGE, CHTHON GLOATS -- BUT IT IS AN EXULTATION SHORT-LIVED. FOR HE HAD UNDERESTIMATED THAT FORCE WHICH SOME HUMANS CALL "GOOD" AND OTHERS CALL "LOVE."
AND THUS THE VERY HEAVENS SHRIEK WITH CHTHON'S ANGER AS HIS ESSENCE IS TORN FORCIBLY FROM ITS NEWLY-CONQUERED VESSEL TO REPLACE THE SOUL OF WANDA FRANK, TRAPPED IN AN EFFIGY OF CARVEN WOOD.

NOOOOO--
--OOOPI--
--IETRO! THE DOLL!

BUT QUICKSILVER'S MIND IS AS QUICK AS HIS FEET!
HE GRABS THE DOLL AND, SPRINTING TO A NEARBY OUTCROPPING--

--FLINGS THAT SEGMENTED HORROR FAR--

--INTO THE SNOW-SWEPT CRATER THAT WAS ONCE GLORIOUS WUNDAGORE!

WANDA! ARE YOU--?
DON'T WORRY, CAP, I'M MY OLD SELF AGAIN-- AND IN MORE CONTROL OF MY POWERS THAN EVER! SO STAND BACK--
--THIS COMBINATION HEX BOLT AND MUTANT BLAST IS GOING TO BRING THE HOUSE DOWN!

YES, THE HOUSE--
SHHHRASSH
--AND HALF A MOUNTAIN!

NO! TH-THIS CAN'T HAPPEN! I'M CHTHON!
CHTHOOOOOOOooo...

IT IS OVER. DJANGO'S MAGIC, AND HIS BELIEF, GAVE US THE KEY.
YES, PIETRO, DJANGO MAXIMOFF SAVED OUR LIVES--
--BY GIVING HIS OWN... WITH A HEART THAT NEVER ONCE STOPPED LOVING US.
SILENCE FOLLOWS... AS DO TEARS.

AND LATER, AFTER EVERYONE HAS GATHERED FOR A SIMPLE, POIGNANT CEREMONY...
HE WAS BURIED IN THE FOREST HE LOVED SO MUCH. I HOPE HE'LL BE HAPPY AT LAST.
I THINK HE WILL BE, WANDA.

BOVA, ARE YOU SURE YOU WANT RESPONSIBILITY FOR MODRED? WITHOUT CHTHON TO GUIDE HIM, HE'S BECOME AS MIND-LESS AS AN INFANT.
I KNOW, CAPTAIN...

...BUT I WAS CREATED TO CARE FOR CHILDREN. I DON'T MIND AT ALL.
THANK YOU, AVENGERS... LET'S GO HOME.
FIN

AVENGERS ASSEMBLE!

c/o MARVEL COMICS GROUP
575 Madison Avenue
New York, New York 10022

ROGER STERN
EDITOR
JIM SALICRUP
ASSISTANT EDITOR

As anticipated, AVENGERS #185-187, featuring (among other things) the origin of Quicksilver and the Scarlet Witch, has become one of the most talked about series of the year, to judge by the volume of fan mail. The funny thing is, even before the book was drawn or written, the series was already causing tremors of excitement around the Marvel offices. Why? Before they even felt ready to sit down and plot, co-plotters Mark Gruenwald and Steven Grant assembled *thirty pages* of single-spaced research into the mutant twins, Wundagore, and the Darkhold. Here, for the first time, is Mark's abridged introduction to the resultant thesis:

"It all began with an attempt to reconcile the mysteries of the origin of Quicksilver and the Scarlet Witch. The earlier version – in which the Whizzer appeared to be their father – didn't account for a number of the puzzle's pieces, not the least of which was why an American named Bob would name his son Pietro. There were other mysterious references: Pietro's vow to his parents (Madeline Joyce died soon after childbirth) that he would care for Wanda, Wanda's comments about being a child during WW2, and Pietro's memories of their father carving marionettes. With a tip-off from John Byrne that a certain well-known Marvel character may have a greater connection to the twins than anyone (himself included) suspected, it was simply a matter then of developing a chronology explaining why two different men claimed to be the father of Wanda and Pietro while a third man actually was.

"In working out that chronology, Steven Grant and I needed a framing device with which to properly tell the story. We found that 'device' in our narrator – the only person who might know the truth about the mutant children (besides their mother) – the midwife: Bova, the evolved cow-woman from GIANT-SIZED AVENGERS #1. But simply having a cow tell a tale does not a story (or even a comic) make. There had to be a conflict. A number of somewhat lame adversaries were rejected by editor Roger Stern, and searches into the Marvel Villains List didn't uncover any indiginous Balkan super-villains. Once again, John Byrne provided the inspiration: The Balkans are a superstitious land; perhaps we should do something moody and atmospheric involving a native demon. That would certainly contrast with the Avengers' usual villainous fare. And so, we began to research native Central European demons and spirits. At first it seemed there weren't any, but then Steven and I discovered that the arcane volume, the Darkhold, was last seen in the Balkans. It had also been in the area a generation earlier, changing the Werewolf by Night's father into a werewolf.

"What if... the Balkan estate of Gregor Russoff, werewolf and scholar, was near the Balkan peak on which Wundagore was built? Wundagore, citadel of evolutionary science, the birthplace of Quicksilver and the Scarlet Witch! The idea was rife with possibilities. And a previous appearance of the Darkhold in the Balkans had occured at about the time of the building of Wundagore! Would the sorcerous forces of the area be affronted by the building of a scientific fortress on the highest peak there? The possible conflict would have been momentous. Soon, after investigating every known appearance of Wundagore and the Darkhold, strange connections – that posed NEW questions – were unearthed. For instance, Spider-Woman was connected to both the Darkhold – having had her past revealed to her by Modred, a sorcerer strongly connected to that book – and to Wundagore, having spent 20 years there in suspended animation. How did Magnus, her later mentor, know so much about her father, scientist Jonathan Drew, one of the builders of Wundagore? Why would a calculating scientist like the High Evolutionary model his New Men after Arthurian knights? The Scarlet Witch started with a scientifically-based mutant hex, but later she was shown to have a significant aptitude for true magic; how was sorcery connected to her mutant birth in Wundagore? Why did her mutant powers fade twice in her career, forcing her to travel back to her native village to reacquire them? What would a particular environment have to do with mutant powers?

"As Steven and I grappled with these questions – and others – some strange patterns emerged. Those patterns seemed so obvious (in retrospect) that it was as if the long list of writers of the Wanda-Pietro saga had been guided by an unseen plan throughout their apparently contradictory works. When we were through making connections, deriving chronologies from fragments, and answering our own questions, we found we had a tapestry that added meaning and depth to a number of pivotal and peripheral characters: Quicksilver, The Scarlet Witch, The High Evolutionary, The Whizzer, Miss America, Bova, Django Maximoff, Jonathan Drew, Gregor Russoff, Spider-Woman, Modred the Mystic, Morgan Le Fay, Magnus, The Knights of Wundagore, The Demon of the Darkhold, and even Merlin himself.

"We also had one weird story."

* * * * * * * *

If the mail is to be believed, The Chthon trilogy was every longtime Marvelite's delight, drawing on more loose plotlines than any other series in memory. For newer readers, who are intrigued by the many years of background on the story – and who would like to know our sources for the information distilled into AVENGERS #185-187 – we present the following bibliography:

Quicksilver and the Scarlet Witch: X-MEN #4, 18, 27; AVENGERS #16, 30, 31, 36, 37, 47, 49, 53, 75, 76, 99, 110, 166, 181, 182; GIANT-SIZE AVENGERS #1; THOR #134; TALES OF SUSPENSE #72.

Wundagore: THOR #134, 135; GIANT-SIZE AVENGERS #1; MARVEL SPOTLIGHT #32; SPIDER-WOMAN #1, 7.

The Darkhold: WEREWOLF BY NIGHT #1, 3, 13, 14, 15; TOMB OF DRACULA #18; MARVEL CHILLERS #1, 2; SPIDER-WOMAN #2, 6; DRACULA LIVES #6.

Last, but not least, we congratulate the many Marvel maniacs who figured out the identity of the true father of Wanda and Pietro from the clues set down in the Wundagore trilogy and in —of all places – X-MEN #125. "So, what's the big deal?" you might ask. "Why don't you just come right out and say that Wanda and Pietro's father is M*gn*t*?"

Because it's a secret, that's why!

You see, it doesn't matter to Wanda and Pietro who their natural father is. They never knew him (as their father). They don't know he is their father. Moreover, the gentleman in question does not know that he ever fathered any children... and there is no way for him to find out! Magda, the children's mother, died somewhere in the mountains near Wundagore, and only she knew the secret. Not even Bova knows the identity of Magda's husband. No one knows... save for you and us and the Watcher!

Far out, eh?

HAVE YOU SEEN THE LATEST
CRAZY?
A 112-PAGE SUPER SPECIAL OF HILARITY AND SURPRISES!
WITH THIS FREE BONUS!
THE ORIGINAL CRAZY COMIC BOOK NO.1... A 32-PAGE FANTASTIC COLLECTORS' ITEM!
ON SALE NOW!

INTERLUDE: A THOUSAND MILES ABOVE THE EARTH, A SQUARE MILE OF ROCK SWINGS TOWARD THE SUNRISE, HIDDEN FROM PRYING EYES BY SOME OF THE MOST SOPHISTICATED ELECTRONICS SYSTEMS EVER CREATED.
THIS IS ASTEROID M... THE HOME OF MAGNETO.

EVER SINCE HIS BATTLE WITH THE X-MEN BENEATH ANTARCTICA, HE'S BEEN HERE NURSING HIS WOUNDS, REGAINING HIS STRENGTH...
0877
MEMORY TAPE 017
...REFINING HIS PLANS TO BECOME MASTER OF THE WORLD.

ABRUPTLY, THE IMAGE ON THE SCREEN BEFORE HIM CHANGES...
MAGDA! BUT HOW--? OH... I SEE.
THE MEMORY CIRCUITS HAVE ACCIDENTLY CROSS-CONNECTED.

MAGDA... MY LATE WIFE. I'D ALMOST FORGOTTEN HOW BEAUTIFUL YOU WERE...

...HOW DEEPLY IT HURT WHEN YOU RAN AWAY FROM ME.
ERASE...

BUT THAT WAS LONG AGO, WHEN I STILL BELIEVED I WAS...
...ONLY HUMAN.
ERASE...

"I AM OLDER NOW, AND I'VE LEARNED MY LESSONS WELL. SOON ALL THE WORLD WILL TREMBLE BEFORE MY POWER!"
BUT MAGNETO ISN'T THE ONLY ONE WITH PLANS AFOOT THIS MORNING--

Magda's unnamed husband was revealed to be Magneto in *X-Men #125* (September 1979), providing the first confirmation that Magneto was the true father of Quicksilver and the Scarlet Witch.

SINCE NOW, YOU BOUNCING BLUE BUFFOON!
CHWUD

CALL OFF YOUR SNAKE, PRINCESS! OR I'LL--
--TURN MY INSIDES TO JELLY? IF I WERE YOU, AVENGER, I'D WORRY ABOUT SOMEONE ELSE'S INSIDES! LIKE--

--MY OWN!

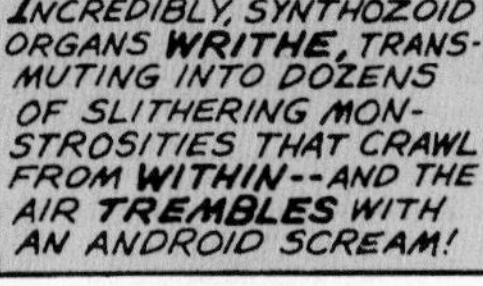
INCREDIBLY, SYNTHOZOID ORGANS WRITHE, TRANSMUTING INTO DOZENS OF SLITHERING MONSTROSITIES THAT CRAWL FROM WITHIN--AND THE AIR TREMBLES WITH AN ANDROID SCREAM!

I DON'T GET IT! PRINCESS PYTHON NEVER HAD SUCH POWERS BEFORE--NOR THE STRENGTH TO STAND UP TO A FULL REPULSOR BLAST!
SHHRAK

WHILE NEARBY...
MISSED, BLAST IT!
KRRITCH
NOT QUITE! WHERE DID NIGHTHAWK GET THOSE TALONS?

HREEEEEE
COVER YOUR EARS, CAP!
THIS SONIC ARROW OUGHT TO PUT A LITTLE SALT ON THAT BIRDIE'S TAIL!

FOOL!
CRACK

Alternate version of *Avengers #182*, page 7

GREG
HORN
2000

Avengers: Nights of Wundagore — *Backpack Marvels* TPB (2000) cover by Greg Horn

To the foreboding land of Transia they have come — the mutants QUICKSILVER™ and the SCARLET WITCH.™ They seek the truth of their deeply hidden heritage; a truth so terrible, the ancient demon CHTHON™ will slay any who dare reveal the secret. "The Yesterday Quest" is a modern masterpiece in the magnificent Marvel Mythos. You must not miss it.
PALMER
ANDREANI

Avengers: The Yesterday Quest TPB (1994) cover by Steve Epting

MARVEL COMICS

EARTH'S MIGHTIEST HEROES!

AVENGERS

THE
YESTERDAY QUEST